TENDER MEDICINE

Touching the Heart, Healing the Hurt

Linda Napier, R.N.

Wing and a Prayer
Press

ISBN 0-9679300-0-6

First Edition
Published by Wing and a Prayer Press
Southbury, Connecticut

Cover concept and art direction by Linda Napier

Cover photography by Jonathan Bodge

Book design by Sharon Hamilton - Women's Publishing, Inc.

The author of this book does not give medical advice nor prescribe the use of any technique for treatment of medical problems. This book's purpose is to offer, from the author's personal and professional experience, information and suggestions that may help you and your doctor, or healthcare provider of your choice, to better work as a team. It is strongly recommended that before using any information in this book, you seek the advice of your healthcare provider. If you decide to use the information contained in this book, you are prescribing for yourself, which is your right under the Constitution, but the author and publisher assume no responsibility for your actions.

For information, address:
Wing and a Prayer Press
657 West Purchase Road
Southbury, Connecticut 06488-1003

To Meagan, precious daughter,
teacher, friend…

…in our quiet understanding,
My love is more than it seems…

The Answer

It faded quietly
In the night,
Parting and slipping away
Like shed skin
Left behind in dreams.
And though yesterday
I had interrogated their eyes,
Their words and mine,
And tortured my brain
Mercilessly,
There were no defectors.
So I surrendered
To the Unknown,
And in the sweep
Of morning's wings,
I knew.

Linda Napier

Contents

PART FOUR
guerrilla nursing

APPENDIX

Learnings and Teachings

Acknowledgments

With Heartfelt Gratitude...

For my petite soeur, my friend, Kiki – I love you.

For Mom and Dad because you loved me with all of your hearts.

For Annie Reuter who, when she worked at Barnes & Noble, told me that because there were no books on this subject, I was "just going to have to write one."

For Jonathan Bodge who encouraged me with his love and confidence in my ability and whose example of focus and determination, when building his house, inspired the completion of this book.

For Laurene Ekse, whose love and guidance where too brief, yet profound.

For Tim Bezler, my favorite ex-husband for your love and support then and now.

For Ed Lynch and his "Healing the Heart" Weekend that forever changed my life.

For all my cherished friends at Adult Children of Alcoholics who loved and accepted all of who I was even when I was unable to love myself.

For all of my wise and wonderful teachers, Marion Rosen, Elaine Mayland, Heather Brown, Sue Brenner and the other instructors and students at the Rosen Institute who so changed the course of my life.

For the staff and counselors at Caron Foundation for their love and support and for my dear friends in the "Best Group", especially my "sister" and "brother" – you both know how much your love meant and still means to me.

For Russ Dunham for being my constant and adoring friend, I adore you, too.

For all of my patients and clients who have become my teachers and my friends, particularly Tony Anthony, Hilary Ben-Ami, Diane Leonard, Barbara Jung, Liz Roberts and Tony Hull. I thank you for the honor of touching you – your trust has moved me deeply. And for the love and memories of Mildred Arnold, Robin Maxwell and Mary Wechter.

For Marcia Brooker, who has decorated my life with her talent and steadfast love – you are a forever friend.

For my sisters in the Women's Leadership Institute at Hartford Seminary for their love and inspiration, especially M.T. Winter, Donna Manocchio, Mary Oliver, Mitzie Monzeglio, Donna Hobbs and Ellie Maher. And for the two "Charter Members" Jan Hendron and Mary Verdosci who had enough faith to buy pre-publication copies of this book – your confidence was motivating!

For my friends who first read the Tender Medicine manuscript and gave me the feedback and encouragement I needed: Bev Dunham, Steven Curry, Vivian Levy, Martha Lopez, Andy Werner, Jill Dougherty, and Mary Boone.

For Tom McDade and Dan Randall whose prolific creativity and uniqueness have been an inspiration to me. Thank you for the love – you have captured my heart.

For Reinhilde Krampe, my dear friend. Your creativity, energy and love of life continually delight and astonish me.

For Linda Bruder for your friendship, confidence, expertise and guidance.

For Tom Atwood, Number One Editor Extraordinaire, for your enthusiasm when I needed it most and for your amazing skills that were so integral to the completion of Tender Medicine. You turned the tide.

For Sharon Hamilton, who knows what living on the edge and taking that leap of faith is all about. Your example gave me that final, gentle nudge and your talents and skills helped pull it all together.

INTRODUCTION

That's it! I'm fed up. After twenty-nine years, I've decided to come out of the closet! No more sneaking around behind closed doors for me. I admit it and I'm not ashamed anymore. I am a registered nurse and I care about my patients! There, I said it! Not only do I care, but I laugh with and cry with, and share with my patients. I touch my patients and hug my patients and even tell my patients that I love them!

I know I'm not alone, either. There are many nurses, doctors, and other healthcare professionals who do the same. It's time that we all step forward, admit that we care and demand that the "heart" be put back in healthcare. I'm all for high tech, but the miracles of modern medicine are hollow when compassion is a low priority in the healing process. The old expression "the operation was a success but the patient died" might easily characterize the state of medicine today.

I'm tired of the whole system, the "medical model" that has coerced me and others like me into hiding our humanity, almost crushing it out of us. It's a system that, for the most part, expects unquestioning obedience and loyalty from both its professionals and its patients. Yet we are people with hearts and souls who have so much to offer toward each other's healing that the system does not allow us to present.

Over the years, I've been a nurse in doctors' offices, intensive care units, medical-surgical floors, rehabilitation hospitals, mental health facilities, convalescent homes and visiting nursing agencies. Many times I've been reprimanded, once even forced out of a job for taking the time to care. We are expected to work like emotionless robots through grueling hours with unsafe nurse to patient ratios and mountains of redundant paperwork. Under these conditions, even maintenance care of patients can barely be done. There is little time for taking a hand, for listening, for caring, for making connections from one human being to another or for shared feelings. House calls from the old family doctor, who was not only health advisor, but confidant and friend have been replaced by the "miracles of modern medicine." "Wonder drugs", sophisticated diagnostic and treatment technology and administrative red tape have further distanced health care professionals from their patients. Satisfaction from a job well done is rare. We mechanically "go through the motions," smile and seem cheerful at best, grumble and are abrupt with patients and colleagues and, at worst, allow ourselves to be set up for making dangerous mistakes. Burnout comes from the impossible expectations that the system puts on us that we dutifully accept.

In modern medicine, there is little time for compassion. From the very beginning of our training, we are advised not to let our feelings get in the way because they will impair our logic and objectivity. We are warned against touching patients lest it be misconstrued as sexual. We are expected to conform. There is little room for humanity in our professional lives and so there is little room for seeing our patients' humanity. At those times when we, as patients, are the most vulnerable, and we, as health-care professionals, are most able to offer the comfort of a compassionate heart, we too often remain isolated and alone. Humanity is seen as only the grit in the oil that lubricates the high-tech modern medicine machine. Now, more than ever, medicine is big business and money is the bottom line.

So now, I am acknowledging my own pain at having given such power and importance to the mainstream medical model, to high-tech medicine, a system whose beginnings sprang from caring. How can it be that good people in a profession with such wonderful ideals have drifted so far from the humanity that we profess to want to serve? My regret is that, for years, I allowed too many of my compassionate words to be silenced, and I did not always offer my gentle touch to someone in pain.

Twelve years ago, I discovered the power of touch in the healing of my own physical pain. Inspired by the profound effect this had on my life,

I learned to touch others in the same way. Touch is quite simple. I gently touch the painful or stressed area of the body with my hands and "listen" to my patient with all of my senses. Quite often, all a person needs is to be listened to, looked at, and touched. Pain needs to be acknowledged. If we deny pain, fighting *not* to feel consumes all of our energy and strength so that there is nothing left for healing and living.

Writing this book will not make up for those missed opportunities to be a gentle presence for another human being. However, the words written here may help other caring healthcare professionals and those on the receiving end of our current system to understand that they are not alone in feeling that major changes need to be made. With the best of intentions, we go into medicine to help people and find that what we have learned in school is not enough. Something is missing that can't be taught...a source of comfort and power derived from our humanity, our compassion, our touch, and our love.

An Act of Congress will not change healthcare. The mainstream medical community with its vast and far-reaching power is a formidable opponent. Those involved in the "business" of medicine – and to many it is only a business – are doing all that they can to ensure that it remains a lucrative, secure, and unchallenged bastion. Healthcare will have to change from the inside out, just as we, as individuals, change within before the change is outwardly evident. As healthcare professionals and patients, we need to ask for what we want and be willing to take a stand. It's about taking responsibility for ourselves and our health. This book is meant to help us to take that first step toward helping ourselves.

As a registered nurse, it is my primary responsibility to take care of myself so that I am able to care for my patients. It means having to say "no" to an unachievable workload and to ask for help when I need it – I'm of no use, and possibly a danger, to my patients, if I'm exhausted and stressed. It also means accepting the fact that as a nurse it is not my job to save the world but I would not be a nurse unless I wanted to help. So whether you are a helping professional, at a loved-one's bedside or simply someone who wants to learn to empower yourself and others, what we can do is to take a hand, "listen" with our hearts to ourselves and others – really "hear" what is being said. No matter what our age, at times we all feel frightened and alone. Touch another as you would a precious newborn. We can say we care, but it's those little acts of love, caring and compassion that will change ourselves first, health-care and then the world.

This book is written in five sections. There may be some parts that will upset you, but I have included them purposely and offer practical, step-by-step summaries that will guide you, or help you to direct someone you know, through similar situations. The first section is about my early years and the circumstances and experiences that influenced me to become a nurse. In the second part, the modern medical system is viewed first hand through my eyes as a nursing student, wanting to save the world, and later as a nurse turned cynic in various mainstream medical settings. The transition, in Part Three, is when I leave nursing, frustrated and disillusioned and, by learning to touch and be touched, begin a relationship with someone I had never known before – myself. The incredible changes that occur with the healing of much of my own physical, emotional and spiritual pain are the start of a new journey for me. Empowered, in Part Four, I return to mainstream medicine, bringing with me my touch and a whole new way of being a nurse. The many wonderful stories about patients that follow demonstrate the profound power of something as seemingly small as being looked at, listened to and touched. Included in the Appendix are practical, step-by-step summaries that will help you to humanize the maze of mainstream modern medicine and empower yourself and others in every area of your life.

We are healed of suffering only
by experiencing it to the full.
—Proust

PART ONE

"...and then I wondered why I had become a nurse in the first place."

Chapter 1

"Mommy, Didn't God Make Doctors, Too?"

Doctor Seynour was a round, red-faced man with a thick neck that swallowed up the ear pieces of his stethoscope. Looking up at him, as a little red-haired, freckle-faced girl, the shiny metal stethoscope appeared to be connected to electrodes on each side of his neck, just like the Frankenstein monster had. The large man wore a stiff, white coat, wielded big needles and was surrounded by all of the same mysterious "doctor" equipment that was surely from Doctor Frankenstein's castle laboratory. Doctor Seynour seemed to be Doctor Frankenstein and the monster all rolled into one. My younger sister, Kiki, and I did not trust him at all and would dutifully say "thank you" for, but would never eat what we believed to be those "doctorized" lollipops he would give us.

It was late summer, time for our annual, school-required physical exams, and our mother was in his examining room with Kiki. Hearing my sister's screams and knowing that I was next, I hid by squiggling under the playpen in the waiting room, then held my breath. The space between the floor and the bottom of the playpen was so narrow that I had to keep my head turned sideways, but could see the adult shoes go by and hear them call my name as they searched everywhere, including the hallways and outside of the big brick building with the maze of walkways and neatly squared hedges. After some time, they stood in the waiting room, discussing their next move. I was counting shoes—shiny black ones with laces (two); my mother's blue canvas sneakers (four); Kiki's red shoes with buckles, like my blue ones (six); the nurse's white ones with wedge heels (eight), then: gray lace-up shoes with swollen ankles that belonged to the lady who answered the phone. I felt outnumbered and started counting again, just to be sure, when someone must have noticed my freckled nose a little too close to the edge of the playpen. They laughed and big hands quickly reached under to pull me out, but I was a quicker "wiggler." Next, the white shoes and the gray shoes with the fat ankles each took an end of the playpen and slid it to the left. I slid to the left. They moved it back to the right, me moving with it. Finally they picked the playpen up while the big hands simultaneously reached under and lifted me up, screaming. The nurse pushed up my sleeve and Frankenstein jabbed my skinny arm with a huge needle.

My mother was a Christian Scientist, who believed in the power of prayer and did not believe in doctors. My father was not a Christian Scientist, wasn't sure about prayer (except in emergencies) and did believe in doctors. Mom was the one, though, who reluctantly took us for our yearly physical exams and immunizations only because they were required by our school and Dad insisted. During those visits to Dr. Seynour, Mom seemed to lose what little confidence she did have and her guilt and fear were palpable. Though Dad was the big, tough World War II veteran, he wouldn't ever take us to the doctor's because, Mom told us, he couldn't stand to hear his little girls cry.

Most of my childhood I had chronic tonsillitis and frequent bouts of strep throat along with stabbing ear infections. Mom would read to me from the *Science and Health* and the Bible, and she would tell me that I was "God's perfect child" and sickness was not a part of that perfection. We would say prayers like the Lord's Prayer and "There's not a spot where God is not for God is everywhere." She would tell me that my sore throat was "Error" and it didn't exist. Spending feverish nights in silence, I was ashamed to let her know that I had allowed "Error" into me again. I had repeated tactile hallucinations: my hands and body were huge and made of rough granite and my bed was a slab of the same cold stone. When I moved, even the slightest bit, the scraping sound jarred me so that my teeth and head would pound and feel stabbed with needles. Breathing would be so hard because my nose was full and my tonsils were so swollen that they touched and just about blocked my throat. Swallowing anything but liquid was impossible and even that was excruciating. "There's not a spot where God is not..."

would remind me of that part of the needlepoint prayer over my friend, Debbie's bed: "...If I should die before I wake, I pray the Lord my soul to take." Those nights were forever, drenched with waking dreams of cold darkness and just as I was sure that I would die, Dad would come into my room in the early morning before leaving for work:

"Jesus, Bette." he'd say in a tremulous voice, his eyes reddened, "Can't you see that your damned prayers aren't working? This child needs a doctor." And because he was big and strong, he could pick up my heavy granite body and carry me to their cool, wide bed, where he would tuck me in and make a phone call. Breathing was easier then and the next time I opened my eyes, Doctor Seynour was at my side, opening his black bag and plugging the stethoscope into the electrodes on either side of his neck. At those times, I saw him like the blind man saw the Frankenstein monster in the movie, not as a scary monster, but as a compassionate listener and friend. He'd give me some pink bubble gum medicine and in a little while, like magic, I'd be thinking about being outside again, playing with my friends.

One afternoon when I was in first grade, I was home from school with another sore throat. Mom sat on my bed reading to me from the *Science and Health* book. I was deep in thought:

"Mommy, is Doctor Seynour a good man?"

"Yes, of course he is," she answered, then continued reading the lesson.

A few minutes later, "Mommy, doesn't God make all good things?"

"Yes, yes of course he does."

"Well, then, didn't God make doctors, too?"

Though I don't remember getting a clear answer from her, there were so many questions that followed that I could never ask. Like, well, if that pink medicine that Doctor Seynour gave me made me feel better, then that was good, and maybe God made that, too.

At a beach party given by some of my Mom's "Christian Science Friends," as Dad called them, I heard a story that I would never forget. Sarah, a big kid, who was twelve, three years older than me, told me about a girl that she used to know from her Sunday school class:

"She died of appendicitis."

"How could that be?" I gasped. "My best friend, Pam, at school, just had appendicitis but she didn't die. Her parents took her to a doctor and she went to the hospital. Pam said it hurt at first, then she was a little sore, but now she's fine."

"Well," Sarah said matter-of-factly, "her parents didn't take her to a doctor and her appendix just burst."

I felt really scared. Sarah's friend probably didn't pray hard enough or good enough or something. Mommy had told me that death is Error and Error is bad. So if God was good, and God was love, why would He let a little girl die? That meant that I could die, too. But then those times when I felt so terrible and Dad had called Doctor Seynour and then I had felt better, well, it was all too confusing.

"Daddy?"I asked the next morning, when the two of us were on our way to Scalzi's, the lumber yard where we began most Saturdays.

"Ummm?"

"How come Mommy doesn't believe in doctors and you do?"

"Because she goes to church with all those nuts."

I thought for a few moments. "Do you believe in God?"

"Yes," he said, clearing his throat as he did when he felt on the spot, "yes I do believe in God."

"And you believe in doctors, too?"

"Yes I do. I believe in God and in doctors."

"Daddy, do you think that God made doctors, too and that they are good like God?"

"Yes...," he said, diddling with the tuning knob on the radio, "I do think that God made good doctors, but though God is always good, not all doctors are good because doctors are people and not all people are good."

"I know that God is always good, but if he's so good, why does he let little girls die?"

Dad cleared his throat again, "What do you mean? Who are you talking about?"

So I told him the story about Sarah's friend and when he heard that she had died of appendicitis, he got pale at first, then red in the face. "God didn't let that little girl die," he said in a loud voice, scaring me a little, "her crazy Christian Science parents did!"

I had all that I could do to keep from crying as I looked out of the car window. My thoughts flew by faster than the white lines on the road and I remembered all of those nights that I'd spent, and feared those I would spend, with sore throats and high fevers sure that I would die.

"What's the matter?" he said in almost a whisper, putting his big hand over mine as it rested limply on the car seat.

"Daddy," I said as bravely as I could, "Daddy, you won't let me die, will you?"

"No, no, Baby, of course not," he said, squeezing my hand and clearing his throat, "Daddy won't let you die."

Chapter 2

"Children: They Pass Thru and On Out..."

It was all very secretive and so it was indirectly I surmised that Mom had to have an operation for what I overheard her tearfully call "a little lump" in her breast.

"I can't believe you've waited so long to have this taken care of, Bette." I overheard Dad say roughly with downcast eyes, "Did you think that you could just pray it away? Jesus, you've known about the lump for two years!"

From my eleven-year-old perspective, it seemed that to Mom, even mentioning any of the "d" words like disease, death or doctors, or to acknowledge the existence of anything other than perfection, was like insuring that those bad things would happen. I got the feeling that she had great guilt over her "failure" and her now scheduled surgery. It was all "hush hush" so as not to "frighten the children," but I sensed her fear. What I found frightening was all of the indirectness and, even more terrifying, that this Christian Science stuff worked like a reverse "three wishes": even thinking about anything negative would cause it to happen. Of course the more I tried not to think something, the more I would think about it.

Sitting in history class on the day of her surgery that I wasn't supposed to know about, I watched the hours creep from one o'clock until school was out, then felt sick riding home on the bus. My head pounded until Dad got home that evening. It was then that Kiki and I were finally "told" about Mom's operation: the doctor had removed the lump and she would be home from the hospital in two days. We talked to Mom later that night on the phone and she reassured us that everything was fine.

After her surgery, though she still did her "lessons," it appeared that Mom was less involved in Christian Science. Maybe it just seemed that way because Kiki and I weren't made to go to Sunday school anymore. We did occasionally go to "Daddy's Church," a Congregational church within walking distance of our house, and joining the Youth Fellowship there, enjoyed the social events that were planned for us as preteens and teens.

Dad had also found a friend in the Reverend Henry Green, a wonderful man from the Midwest , who was more like a farmer than a minister. Born and raised in the hills of Kentucky, my Dad, Arlis, was a "country boy" himself so he had a lot in common with Henry. They would compare notes on their vegetable gardens and together they began an annual fall tradition of making homemade applesauce from Dad's apple harvest. Mom was also very fond of Henry and so for the next several years, it seemed that there was less religious tension, and whenever I had a sore throat, I was taken to Dr. Seynour for antibiotics.

Dad continued binge drinking, something that only then, as a teenager, I was finally able to see as the cause of his frequent rages and erratic behavior. For as long as I could remember, though, I had always felt that when I was with him, I was walking on eggshells. Somehow I knew the unwritten rule: "Don't hurt Daddy's feelings." Though he stood over six feet tall, he seemed so easily wounded. Dad's family had always called me "Little Arlis" because they said I was so much like my father. Mom used to tell me that I understood him better than anybody else. It was in my teen years that on many occasions I would find Dad drunk on the floor or passed out in his car. I'd help him to bed if I could, or cover him with a blanket if I couldn't and would all too often clean up his vomit or broken dishes and food he'd thrown. Still, he owned a successful ad agency in New York City and we lived in a nice home with a swimming pool and had all of the "advantages" of an upper middle class family.

Five years after her operation, Mom went into the hospital again. The cancer had spread and this time they did a right radical mastectomy followed by radiation therapy. I was sixteen, when she confided in me, saying she didn't want to upset Kiki. I felt both honor that I was "trusted" and horror as she showed me her mutilated chest where her right breast had been. There were red marker "target" lines for her radiation treatments. "I'm not a woman anymore," she wept.

From that point on, I noticed that Mom was back into her Christian Science full force, doing her lessons every day, going to church and Wednesday night meeting and regularly seeing a practitioner who would work with her on "clearing her thoughts so she could heal." I am sure, however, there was no mention of her surgery or other medical treatments.

About a year after her mastectomy, I went with Mom to see her oncologist, Dr. Rossberg. After he had examined her, we sat in his office, where he looked over some test results. My heart pounded and I felt queasy.

"Well, Bette," he began after sighing and clearing his throat, "I think it's time to begin you on some chemotherapy."

Her chin trembled. "What do you mean? Why I thought everything was fine..."

"Now, now Bette, I never said that. But we need to start you on chemotherapy," he said as if he were speaking to a child.

"Dr. Rossberg," she blurted, eyes filling with tears, "Please tell me about this chemotherapy. I'm not sure that I want to have it."

"Now you listen to me," he said gruffly, "you don't have a choice. If you don't do as I say you're going to die."

As Mom's body began to weaken, there was a metamorphosis. Her hair had turned a brilliant silvery-white in only a year, her eyes sparkled, her cheeks glowed. She seemed to be looking at life for the first time and found it precious. Living day to day with wonder in all things, she immersed herself totally in her art which she loved. Seizing the moment for the first time in her life, she traveled and ate exotic foods with zest. I had always loved my mother, but in the past, she had been intense, fearful and often preoccupied. To be with her now was a joy. She was my confidante, my sounding board with whom I could share my dreams, loves and failures, the mother that I had always wanted, encouraging me to follow my dreams.

After spending a near semester at Stephen's College, a Missouri liberal arts college for women and Mom's alma mater, then taking a few odd jobs while living back at home in Connecticut, I decided to go to the "Coast" in the spring of 1970. With twenty-four dollars and a one-way student stand-by ticket in my backpack, I stood on the porch with Mom. The sunlight was dazzling her silver hair, though today she seemed thinner and her cheeks lacked color. We hugged tearfully.

"I love you," she said softly, pressing an envelope into my hand. "Open this when you're on the plane."

"Is there anything I can do for you before I go?"

She paused, then said suddenly, "Yes, don't go."

"What? Really?"

"No, no, I didn't mean that. I want you to go. You have to live your life."

I felt myself waver, "Mom, I'll stay, if you want me to."

"No, go! I love you. Go now and open the envelope on the plane!"

With New York City below me, I opened the white envelope and found a fifty dollar bill and a poem Mom had written:

> Children
> They pass thru
> and on out.
> Straight if you let them
> Or all twisted if you don't.

If you smile as they pass,
They grow taller
If not, they crawl close to the ground
They must pass thru one way or the other...

Though I had loved California and my new friends, six months later I was back home again in Greenwich. Worry about Mom had too often distracted me and I knew I had to be with her.

When I was a little girl and people asked me what I wanted to do when I grew up, I had always said without hesitation, "I want to help people." Being a nurse had always been in the back of my mind, but I don't remember ever expressing that out loud. But now I was in nursing school, officially learning to do what I had done all of my life: take care of people.

Anatomy and physiology, chemistry, microbiology all those maths and sciences had always been a struggle for me, but I loved the psychology, philosophy and writing classes. Our clinical instruction was at the hospital where Mom had had her surgery and next to Dr. Rossberg's office.

One day after class, I was walking down to the hospital parking lot with my friends when I saw Dad's car stopped in the middle of the drive. Mom had her head hanging out of the open door and was retching.

"Oh, no," I said to my friends as I left them, "Mom's had chemotherapy again today."

Dad was sitting stiffly behind the wheel, looking straight ahead, as Mom clung onto the door handle in a cold sweat, the veins on her forehead and neck bulging. When she stopped vomiting and seemed a little better, Dad drove her right home and I followed in my car.

Then as now, I wonder at the logic of chemotherapy and radiation in end stages of cancer. Though they said it was for "comfort measures" and Mom had been scared into obeying her doctor, those many times when I held her head as she retched into the toilet after chemotherapy and when I saw the blackened and shriveled chest from radiation, I wasn't so sure.

Every day, after school, I would cleanse her ulcerated and oozing chest and apply new bandages and tell her that they were looking better, though they were only getting worse. She was much weaker and finally had to be put back into the hospital. A lung had collapsed and she was unable to eat. Her beautiful teeth stretched gaunt lips. She looked like a bewildered little bird.

Her Christian Science practitioner refused to visit her in the hospital, but would speak to her over the phone about the non-existence of disease and pain and warned her about "clouding her thinking with pain medications."

Dad and I took turns staying in Mom's hospital room each night on a cot and one night when I arrived after classes I found her crying in pain.

"Mom, did you have your pain shot?"

"No, no, no," she squeaked hoarsely between rapid gulps of air, "I can't have any of that stuff, it clouds my thinking."

"Mom, if you had at least some you might feel better. How about a half of a dose? That won't be as strong, but you'll feel a little better."

She argued a bit more with me then finally agreed to a half of a dose.

Thrilled, I ran down the hall to the nurse's station to let her nurse know that Mom wanted a half dose of her Demerol.

"I'm sorry," she said, "but the doctor has ordered fifty milligrams of Demerol."

"Well, she wants twenty-five."

"I can give her fifty or nothing."

"What?" I growled.

"I'm sorry, but what am I supposed to do with the other twenty-five?"

"Waste it!" I hissed, "Or better yet, take it yourself!"

Shortly, after Mom got her half dose, she rested more comfortably while I sang Christian Science hymns to her until she slept.

The next day, I made an appointment with Mom's Christian Science practitioner, Mrs. Williamson, an elderly heavy-set woman. I had all I could do to contain my anger and rehearsed what I wanted to say over and over while driving to her house.

"Hello dear," she smiled as she opened the door, "I'm so glad to see you."

"I won't take up much of your time, or mine," I began, as we both perched on the edges of the uncomfortable chairs in her formal living room, "but I need to talk to you about my Mom. First of all, I think it's bad enough that you refuse to visit her in the hospital..."

"Well, dear," she interrupted, "we don't like to give power to the ills of the body, to Error, and a hospital is full of negative thoughts."

"If you're right, and your thoughts are always positive, then what are you afraid of?"

"I'm not afraid. I don't give any power to Error," she said as if she were speaking to a child.

"By your denial you are. By abandoning your client when she is in the most need, you are. But let me get to my point. Mom thinks you and Christian Science can heal her and I have to honor her wishes, but personally," and I felt myself begin to tremble, my face flush, "personally, Mrs. Williamson, I want to know where you get off standing in judgment of another human being? I want to know what gives you the right to tell her that she shouldn't take pain medication when you sit here healthy and alive and she's lying in a hospital with tubes draining her chest because she's literally drowning in fluid, and full of terrible pain! You are not facing death and constant pain, what right have you to increase her fear and guilt?"

"I only told her that drugs would cloud her thinking."

"And you don't think that excruciating physical pain also clouds thinking?"

"I'm so sorry that you feel this way, dear."

"Please," I said, so enraged that I couldn't contain the tears that ran down my face, "don't call me 'dear'. My name is Linda." and with that I got up and left her house.

It was on a rainy morning in early December of 1971 that Mom died. If death was seen as "Error" to the Christian Scientists, it seemed like a blessing to me. But the blessing only went as far as an end to her suffering. I still couldn't understand why she had to die and the empty space in my life where she had been felt too vast to endure. My sister, father and I seemed to be orbiting even farther apart then ever and we wallowed in quiet distance coping as best as we knew how.

Kiki and I had a screaming fight, something we hadn't done since our early teens, when we were going through Mom's clothes and personal effects. My sister wanted to linger over each item while I wanted to give everything to Goodwill.

"Get rid of it." I'd say for each dress or sweater.

"No! No, how could you want to throw her things away?" she'd cry.

Meanwhile Dad, who had found solace in drinking and in an affair he'd been having with Mom's best friend, went off to Puerto Rico with her, thinking we had no idea what was going on.

It wasn't until eight years later that I was finally able to grieve the loss of my mother. She had requested to be cremated and Dad and Henry, the minister, had scattered her ashes up at "Daddy's Church," but there had been no marker. It was at this time that I felt that I needed a place to go to feel closer to her, so I talked with Kiki and we decided to have one of her poems put on a bronze plaque. Mom had always loved pink dogwoods so we planted one with the plaque at its base which read:

True being never ceases,
Endlessly a smile, a single word,
Recalled in Love and Life
Renews itself...

Bette Napier 1923-1971

CHAPTER 3

"BABIES DON'T FEEL ANY PAIN..."

In the classroom, everything was neat and clean and bound up in crisp books. There were techniques and nursing approaches and rationale. There were care plans and everything seemed to make perfect sense. Adding one necessary ingredient, real live patients, who didn't always go "by the book" seemed to shake all of us up. Our class lost a good percentage of its students, who dropped out soon after we started our clinical training, the actual hands-on learning. Nursing and modern medicine wasn't as glamorous, perfect or noble as it seemed to be on Marcus Welby, M.D., a popular T.V. show.

A dinner party at eight

Sandy had been in labor most of the night and I was her assigned student nurse for the day. She said it had been mild labor and she was very excited and happy about having natural childbirth. Sandy and her husband, Gary had taken LaMaze classes together in joyful anticipation of their first child but because she was not fully dilated and her labor was going slowly, he had gone home to get some sleep. Her labor dragged on, with very few contractions, but I enjoyed spending time with her, one on one. As students, we usually were assigned one or two patients and we could give them lovely hours of undivided attention.

After lunch, out at the nurse's station, I overheard Sandy's doctor talking to the head nurse:

"Sally," he said hurriedly, "let's give Sandy some Pit to see if we can't hurry things along. I have a dinner party this evening at eight. If she doesn't deliver soon, we'll do a C-section at three."

When I returned to Sandy's room, she was crying. "Doctor Gibb just left. He wanted me to sign permission to do a Caesarean Section but I told him that I wanted to do LaMaze. He got really upset with me and left abruptly, saying he'd be back at two. They're going to give me an IV with some medicine that will help my labor."

I wanted to tell her to refuse the Pitocin and let nature take its course, but I couldn't. We had been warned that a nurse, especially a student nurse, should never question a doctor's decision, and most of all never let a patient know that you don't agree with a doctor.

So as the Pitocin made Sandy's contractions stronger and stronger, even though she wasn't fully dilated, her pain increased. Imagine the uterus pushing the baby harder and harder against a half closed opening. By the time Dr. Gibb returned several hours later, Sandy was begging for a C-section. She had major surgery for what could have been a natural birth with Gary at her side, and the doctor made his dinner party on time.

When I talked to my instructor, she reiterated what we had already been told many times in the classroom: you never question a doctor. When I told her I wanted to report the doctor, she asked me who I would report him to? The hospital administrator or one of his other peers? Would the nurse that he had spoken to verify what I heard? The doctor would probably deny it. "This is off the record, but they all stick together, you'd never be able to prove it." Infuriated, I began to lose my respect for modern medicine that day. As time went on, I tended to forget that these were separate incidents and individual doctors and they all weren't like him. Having been forewarned by my instructor, I never went to a higher authority or spoke with the patient. Today, I would do it differently.

"There's nothing more that can be done for you..."

As a student on a medical-surgical floor, I was often assigned to care for post-operative patients. One afternoon, I was entering the room of a

patient who had just had exploratory abdominal surgery, I saw that the doctor was with her. Because he was standing at the the end of her bed, as if he were about to leave, I waited at the door.
"Florence," he said sharply, almost angrily, "I'm afraid I have some bad news."

She looked up at him fearfully, and tears filled her eyes. She caught herself and took a deep breath.

He didn't wait for her to respond, "We found your abdomen to be full of cancer. There is too much and it's inoperable." The surgeon's eyes only met hers briefly once or twice, then they searched the yellow walls of the room. "There is nothing more that can be done for you. I'm sorry."

Florence let out a little gasp then began to cry softly. The doctor shifted from foot to foot, cleared his throat and repeatedly clicked the pen in his hand before glancing over at me. Then he looked at his watch, silently turned and left the room.

I stood momentarily horrified and enraged at what I had just seen, then went to her and wrapped her in my arms. I had wanted the doctor to DO something for Florence, to "make it better" and of course, he couldn't. Though I'm sure he had his own issues around death and his feelings of failure to deal with, it was, as I saw it, the patient who was abandoned by her doctor. What made me more angry was that I felt like I had gotten stuck with his mess: there I was, left to deal with a no-win situation and I felt inadequate and untrained to help this woman.

"Babies don't feel any pain..."

When I did my training in the newborn nursery, I was asked to assist a doctor as he did a circumcision. There was a little fiberglass mold that was shaped to hold an infant with little velcro straps to pin his wrists and ankles down. It looked like a torture rack and the different devices used for circumcision were stainless steel and had names like the "guillotine." When the little one was strapped into the restraint, he screamed. When the circumcision was done, his scream became a shrill wail. The procedure was done without any sedation or even local anesthesia. When I asked the doctor why nothing was used, he replied, "Babies don't feel any pain, he's just screaming because he's restrained."

I've often thought about that day – of course babies feel pain! Another similar belief was that the elderly didn't feel the heat and so most older convalescent homes didn't have air-conditioning. This, I guess, was just another straw on the camel's back of insensitivity in the modern medical setting, that added to my feelings of cynicism. With a sigh, I must have thought, "You can't fight city hall..." and "When in Rome..." of course the Romans fed people to the lions for entertainment, didn't they?

"Welcome to the Nut House!"

Our psychiatric clinical training was done at a state psychiatric hospital. The first time I walked onto the locked ward huddled with a small group of student nurses, there were several patients sitting around a large table in the day room rolling state-issued tobacco in rolling papers. Alice, a woman in her late fifties wearing excessive makeup so she looked like a clown, must have seen our apprehension. She jumped up and threw open her arms: "Welcome to the Nut House!" she screamed raucously. Then she began to dance around singing "I'm out of my tree, I'm out of my tree..." in a sing-songey way. I did get to know Alice because she was my assigned patient and when we later talked about that first day, she admitted that she had done that performance for our benefit.

One of many things that I learned from her was that she and many others, knew exactly how to play the system. When Alice would come up for review and she had decided she wanted to be released, she knew just what to say and do to get out. Alice used to laugh about all of those "self-important and pompous psychiatrists and therapists," with their piles of papers who thought they were making the decisions. "But that's okay," she'd say, "let em think what they want because I'll be out of here, you mark my words." And sure enough, the next week, Alice would have been discharged. When she needed to come back into the facility, there she'd be, waiting for me with her big I-told-you-so smile. So there went some of my confidence in the psychiatrists, who cleared their throats and shuffled papers, while many patients, who had been committed because they were "mentally incompetent," decided when they would be admitted and discharged.

One day, I came onto the locked ward and into the day room. I had thought "Cuckoo's Nest" day rooms were only in the movies, but this one was exactly like the film's right down to the color of the walls. There were many patients milling around, a small group sitting at the table smoking, when suddenly I heard a high-pitched wail that was so full of anguish that tears immediately filled my eyes. I looked around quickly to see a woman, no older than my twenty-one years, as she began to bang her head against the large concrete pillar in the day room. There were no other students with me and no staff in sight.

She screamed again to the universe and no one in particular, "You want me to hurt someone! You want me to hurt myself!" as she continued slamming her head against the pillar. The sound of her skull as it hit the concrete made me move toward her. She was smaller than myself and I planned to pull her back away from the pillar. But as I approached, she turned and started heaving furniture. One piece, a huge upholstered sofa, she flung as if it were a cigarette butt. As I halted in my tracks to reconsider, the staff must have finally heard the commotion from the break room and came in to restrain the woman as she continued to scream and curse everyone and no one.

I cried when I left the ward and my instructor took me aside for a conference. She wanted to know why this had touched me so deeply and I honestly didn't know. Perhaps, I told her, it was because I felt so badly for the patient and what she must have been going through. My instructor said that we all have the exact same feelings and that it was only a matter of degrees of intensity that separated the sane from the insane. I didn't find that too comforting and driving home that afternoon, I cried so much that I had to stop on the side of the road several times.

What I wasn't aware of then was that that patient had touched my own pain that I held so deeply inside of me, so deeply, that I was totally unaware of it until years later.

"That's the alcohol talking..."

Working on a detox ward, I knocked, unlocked the door and entered the room. She looked at me with the hostility and fear of a startled beast. Thick lenses magnified her wounded eyes and the rims of her glasses were the same red color as her shapeless lips. The remains of a chocolate milkshake had dried around her large mouth, making it appear to have been smeared over most of her face. Something white was caked in her brown, matted hair and here and there large tufts stuck straight up. Her head was supported by several chins which turned into great folds and then into mounds of yellow flesh.

She snorted as I approached the bed. My shoe soles stuck to that same chocolate milkshake that had dried around her mouth, on top of and in drips down the side of the night table and in finger prints on the sheets and bed rails. The stench in the room was a combination of urine, body odor and a night stand drawer full of hoarded, rotting food.

When she screamed, "Get the hell out and leave me alone!" I could smell the alcohol and vomit on her breath. She had been here many times before and so had I.

I found her repulsive and had no patience for alcoholics or drug addicts and though the "medical model" told me that addiction is a disease, I had a lot of trouble with that idea. My father had been a binge drinker for years and the abuse that my mother, sister and I endured because of it was inexcusable. Mom used to always say, "That's not Daddy, that's the alcohol talking." Well, it sounded like Dad to me and after all, he drank the alcohol, didn't he? It wasn't forced down his throat.

On several other occasions, as a nurse working with detoxing patients, I have been subjected to verbal and physical abuse. Back then, I did my job and tried to show compassion for the person.

One particular day, in the intensive care unit, I was assisting a doctor as he was giving blood transfusions and ice water lavage to an alcoholic patient who was bleeding from his whole gastrointestinal tract. The patient was calling me the worst possible names and hit and clawed me until we restrained his hands. As fast as the blood was transfused in, it was coming out of his rectum and I couldn't clean him quickly enough to keep him from sitting constantly in a pool of blood. I was angry at being verbally and physically abused when I was only trying to help him and I wondered why they just didn't let him die, because it seemed like that's what he wanted.

Later, in the nurse's station, I suggested to the doctor that we just recycle the blood he was sitting in and he said that if we could invent a way to make it reusable, we'd be rich. That night, the patient died.

All I could do was love her...

Two little blonde girls lingered by their mother's hospital room door, as their father ran to me: "My wife is getting sick. do something!"

My first reaction was one of repulsion and emotional self-preservation. Earlier that morning I had been relieved to find that this thirty-seven year old woman in the terminal stages of lung cancer had been assigned to another student nurse. I had avoided entering her room all day and now that my shift was ending, I had to decide.

Caring for patients with cancer stirred up those memories of my mother's slow death which I had tried to forget : the odor of disintegrating flesh as it became ulcerated and oozing; the excruciating pain brought on by a movement, the touch of a sheet or from deep within the frail skeleton; the bewildered terror in drug-glazed eyes.

I could still feel the nauseating anger that I felt then. I loved her and there was no one who loved me as she did and yet, there I was, healthy and strong and I could do nothing! I wanted to save her, to soothe her and all I could do was love her and it didn't seem like enough.

"Do something!" he urgently repeated.

I considered calling the student who had been put in charge of her care for that day, stopped, took a breath and approached the door.

She looked up at me and her head wavered as if she were a delicate baby bird just lifting its head for the first time. White eyeballs and teeth protruded from the taut skin over that skeletal bewildered face.

The intensity of her pain had made it impossible for her to eat anything. Her frail body shuddered with the pain and the violence of her vomiting. There was nothing I could do. Anything I would do would seem so small and useless against such devastation.

After inserting a compazine suppository to relieve her nausea, I put a cold washcloth on her forehead and stroked her head until her nausea subsided. Powerful drugs had caused her hair to fall out and now just a fine fuzz remained.

As we waited for the medication to ease her pain, I rubbed her back, feeling each vertebra as I smoothed on the lotion.

"It made me feel so good to see my girls today..." her voice trailing off and quivering.

We talked about her girls, their school, those things they loved to do, their lives and she was lost in other times. As I gently rubbed her back, I felt the tension leave her. She smiled faintly and her eyes closed into quiet sleep.

Though a part of me sensed then, that I had done what I could, it didn't seem like enough. There should have been something that I could have done or said that would have been better. Being with dying people was frightening because it seemed that on some level, I had failed them.

Human error

It was my day to pass medications to the patients on a med-surg floor in the hospital where we did our clinical training. With my instructor looking over my shoulder, the medications for each patient were poured into a small cup after carefully checking the medication, route and dosage against the patient's medication record. On this particular patient, the medication I was giving was Coumadin, a blood thinner, which was ordered to be given every other day. That day, he was not supposed to have it, but neither my instructor nor I noticed the error until he had already swallowed the pill. I felt terrible when we discovered it, but fortunately, it had no ill effects on the patient. The error had to be reported to the patient's doctor and the director of nurses. The doctor was only mildly interested and asked that the medication be held the next day and then resumed as ordered. My instructor and I were asked to report to the Director of Nurses office:

"How did this happen?" she demanded.

I was on the verge of tears, "I don't know."

"What do you mean you don't know?"

"I'm sorry." I said softly.

"Human error," my instructor interjected matter of factly.

"What?" said the surprised DNS.

"I said human error," repeated my instructor.

"That's not good enough."

"Well, it'll just have to be good enough. It happens..."

Before that incident, I had always worried about making a mistake. After that, the thought terrified me. It seemed to me like the Director of Nurses was saying that as a nurse, you had to be perfect, mistakes were inexcusable. Though I had always been careful with all that I did, checking and double checking, after that I was afraid to ask because I didn't want to look like a fool. I thought I was supposed to know it all, even as a student and if I didn't, nobody would know. I was reassured, at least consciously, by telling myself that my mistakes were small and inconsequential compared to the others that I'd witnessed or heard about.

Once, as a student, I was assisting in the operating room when the surgeon, who had an excellent reputation, said suddenly under his breath, "Damn!"

The scrub nurse asked, "What is it?"

Whistling, his green mask bellowed, "Nothing like taking a blind stab near the heart," he laughed tightly. "It's okay, though, everything looks fine," he said seemingly more to reassure himself than anyone else.

Another time I heard, from some staff and students in the hospital, that a young woman with two small children, came in for what should have been a routine surgical procedure. The anesthesiologist got the gasses switched and she suffered permanent brain damage, so severe that she was a "vegetable" and had to be institutionalized.

Autopsies were optional

Then there was Julia Africa and though it's been many years, I remember her name clearly. She took her last breath with me sitting by her side and death came so gently to her after eighty-eight years, twelve grandchildren and seven great-grandchildren, that a whisper would have been a roar. I knew about her life and her family and loved the time we'd spent together, and though she'd told me that she was ready to die, I could not believe that anyone should be ready to die. But it was I who was not ready then to touch those painful places in me. Still, she was my first teacher on the art of dying with dignity and grace.

Autopsies were optional for nursing students, but since I wanted to experience it all and because most of the other students were going, I found myself in the hospital morgue. The body was that of an elderly female, pasty-colored flesh on a stainless steel table with small perforations in it. I shivered and thought about how cold she must be, naked on the icy table. When the pathologist began making incisions, he hosed out the cavities with water and diluted body fluids trickled through the perforations in the table to the tray below. He matter-of-factly removed organs, hosing them off and holding them up for us to see, describing any abnormalities he noted. Then he cut through her rib cage with a little circular saw. It sounded like he was cutting a chicken apart. I shivered again, feeling queasy but trying to convince myself that this woman was feeling no pain and this was a way to learn. Then something caught my attention: I had moved to a different spot and was horrified to see that the woman on the table was my sweet patient, Julia Africa. Feeling sick, I turned and left the cold room.

I couldn't stand to see Julia dead because I had known her in life and it seemed like she was was being butchered like a cow. Death seemed unnatural, a failure and reminded me too much of the black space in my gut that was left after Mom died.

But that may have been a rumor

The state boards for nursing licensure were held in July in Hartford and those three days the thermometer hovered it the 103 degree area. The armory where the exams were held was even hotter than outside because of the skylight windows streaming sunlight in from above. We all wore bathing suit tops and shorts, bringing ice buckets and wash-cloths from the hotel. Every once in awhile, there would be a crash, as one of the graduate nurses would pass out and fall to the floor. We called the local T.V. station who covered the story and I understand that a year or two later, and since then, the nursing boards were held in air-conditioned comfort, but that may have just been a rumor.

In spite of my growing cynicism, I guess I thought that my graduation and transition into nursing would be special and in many ways it was. I was proud of me, though even then, I had started wondering why I had chosen nursing as a career. Modern medicine was far from perfect and pink "bubble gum" medicine couldn't always make things better. There was a part of me, ever-hopeful and optimistic that the experiences that had begun to harden me, were only those of a student. As soon as I became a real nurse, I told myself, things would be different because then I could make a difference...

Things which matter most must
never be at the mercy of things
which matter least.
—Goethe

PART TWO

inside the mainstream modern medical machine

Chapter 4

The Real World

It was the fall of 1973 and the war in Viet Nam was, they said, "winding down." Bob, my husband, a private in the Army and one of the "last of the draftees," was stationed at Schofield Barracks on the island of Oahu, Hawaii. He had graduated from college with a degree in mechanical engineering, so it made perfect military sense that he was trained in San Antonio, Texas, to be a medic then assigned to be the captain's driver at Schofield Barracks.

My first job was at a doctor-owned hospital and clinic on the island. The facility was a thirty-bed hospital that had a small emergency room, operating room and delivery room. It also had an ambulance and two male attendants who were also supposed to serve as orderlies for the hospital if it didn't interfere with their card games. The clinic, which also had a pharmacy, catered mostly to the locals, many of whom were on welfare. Besides the original Hawaiian people, the population also consisted of Samoans, Phillipinos, Japanese, some American civilians and the American Military, who only appeared when large doses of penicillin were in order.

The head nurse at the hospital was named Suzanna. Her husband was a captain so she believed she had rank, too. We'd sometimes car pool to work together, but we didn't have much in common.

"So I bought this dress for the officer's party and when I showed it to my husband, he didn't like it," she said one morning on our way to work.

"But you liked it, otherwise you wouldn't have bought it, right?"

"Well, yeeess," she said in her slow, hesitant way.

"So if you like it and feel good in it then wear it!"

"No, I'm returning it."

"Then is he going shopping with you to pick out another?"

"Oh, no. He would never go shopping," she said blankly.

"I don't understand it. What if he doesn't like the next one you buy?"

"Then I'll keep trying until he likes one."

"I dress to please myself," I said emphatically.

"Well, I dress only to please my husband," she replied vaguely, like I wasn't even there.

I nicknamed her "Suzanna Banana", though not to her knowledge, of course. Don't know why, exactly but it just seemed to fit her.

One morning, a young Samoan woman was admitted in labor with her first child. She was transferred into the delivery room and when I went in to greet her, I found she spoke very little English. She seemed to indicate that her family may be on their way. I did a complete assessment then found her cervix to be fully effaced and five centimeters dilated, which meant that she was halfway to full dilation and pushing the baby down the birth canal. This I reported to Suzanna Banana.

"Wellll," she said deliberately before sipping on her coffee, "since this is her first baby, she'll take a long time so we won't need to call the doctor for hours...." she said more to the chart on the desk in front of her than to me.

After about twenty minutes, when I returned to prep her, Sepella appeared much more uncomfortable, though she smiled calmly when I entered the room. The fetal heart rate was fine, hers was up and her contractions were good and strong. Better check her dilation, I thought. I was truly surprised to find her just about fully dilated and quickly returned to the nurse's station to tell Suzanna to call the doctor.

"No," she said, looking past me, "It's way too soon."

"She's just about fully dilated," I insisted.

"It's impossible."

"You need to call the doctor."

"And I say NO! Remember who's in charge here."

"Okay, but..."

"Do you want me to report you for insubordination?"

I was boiling, but I stuffed it and returned to Sepella. She looked alarmed and I started to check her again but her vulva was bulging, the bed was wet where her water had broken and she was bearing down. I pulled the call light, grabbed some sterile gloves and put them on, just as the head with wet, curly hair emerged into my waiting hands. Another push and Sepella had a lovely baby girl. It was about that time that an annoyed Suzanna huffed into the room only to stop dead in her tracks and drop her jaw.

"Will you please bring the suction over here?" I said, trembling from the excitement and fear of my first solo delivery and anger towards Suzanna. Though I guess I should have been used to it by then, I hated being put into positions that I was unprepared for. I was grateful that everything seemed to have turned out well in spite of my inexperience. Suzanna silently suctioned the child as I held her until her breaths became clear, then I wrapped her in a blanket and placed her into Sepella's waiting arms.

"I'm calling the doctor," Suzanna said as she turned and hurried from the room.

John was a Hawaiian man in his late twenties who was admitted for a fractured femur. Dr. Meyerson, one of the owners of the hospital-clinic, had put the man in traction. I never could understand why he hadn't casted him and nobody seemed to have an answer. Dr. Meyerson would always get angry if anyone ever dared question his judgment. It didn't occur to me until later, that Dr. Meyerson could make more money if John was an inpatient than if he had been casted and sent home with crutches. So the weeks went on and John remained in traction, a pin through his knee, attached to pulleys and weights. One day, while helping him with a bed bath, I noticed that there was a lump on the top of his thigh of the fractured leg, which I reported to Suzanna Banana. She just shrugged and didn't answer.

A few weeks later I spoke with her again:

"Suzanna, why can't we just get Dr. Meyerson to order another x-ray of John's femur? He hasn't had one since the day he was admitted and that was over six weeks ago!"

"Linda," she said with a sigh, "The doctor knows what he's doing more than you or I. Didn't you learn that in nursing school?"

I waited until that Sunday, when both Suzanna and Dr. Meyerson were not working and spoke to Dr. Tanichi about it. He agreed that we needed an x-ray and since our x-ray tech was on call for emergencies only, the doctor and I took John down for the film.

After a short time, he called me into his office. John's x-ray was up on his light box. Dr. Tanichi shook his head then he silently nodded toward it. The femur was completely broken in two with the ragged end of the lower portion jutting up against the soft tissue of John's mid thigh.

"There's no excuse for this," I said angrily.

"You're right and we'll take him into surgery tomorrow first thing."
"How are you going to explain this to John?"

"Don't worry, we'll handle it. Oh, and Linda, for your own good, let us handle it. There's no need to mention this to anyone, if you know what I mean."

Both Dr. Tanichi and Dr. Meyerson performed surgery, but only Dr.

Tanichi was skilled as a surgeon, though he was often sarcastic and flip with patients and staff. Dr. Meyerson was an American in his early sixties, cocky and aloof. Sloppy and forgetful both professionally and personally, he was the controlling shareholder of the hospital/clinic. One of his patients, a woman in her early forties had come in for an appendectomy and was found dead in her bed a few days post op. Ask as I did, nobody ever seemed to know the cause of her death and her chart had already been taken from the nurse's station when I looked for it.

After about six months of working in the hospital with Suzanna as head nurse, my request for a transfer to the adjoining clinic was granted. There I assisted the three doctors with examinations and procedures and filled prescriptions. On any given day, the lanai or wide, open-air porch which served as the waiting area, was filled to overflowing with many people, most of whom were on welfare. The large majority of them would come for colds and minor injuries that really didn't require a doctor's visit, but Dr. Meyerson would be sure that all were seen. After antibiotics were ordered and dispensed for the colds, and the cuts and scrapes were cleansed and bandaged, the bill was sent to Uncle Sam. The clinic was always packed and very busy with each of the three doctors seeing five to six patients an hour. Dr. Meyerson had a large following of overweight patients for whom he prescribed weekly injections of Ritalin which, he told them, would make them lose weight. As the nurse who administered the medication and weighed them in each week, the results were negligible. He rarely gave these patients more than a quick hello and his recommendations for diet, stress management and exercise were vague at best, but usually nonexistent. He also had a multitude of "depressed" or "nervous" patients who would come in every month for a "check up" and to get their Valium or other medications refilled at the clinic pharmacy. There was never any psychotherapy for these patients, just the medication that Dr. Meyerson, who was a general practitioner, would prescribe.

Several years after Bob and I returned to Connecticut, I received a letter and request for any information I might have, from an attorney representing the family of a patient of Dr. Meyerson's. It seemed that this patient had been admitted to the hospital with a psychiatric diagnosis, though there was no psychiatrist on staff. One night, the patient, who was very agitated, wandered from his room out onto the grounds, fell down a steep embankment onto the road and died.

CHAPTER 5

LOOKING FOR MS. "GOODJOB"

Marjorie sat in the swivel chair at her desk with coffee and Danish, as her ample body and generous folds that strained against her white uniform spilled over the seat sides and from under its back. She was talking on the phone to a patient, asking about symptoms and giving medical advice.

"Mmmmhuh," she said, swallowing a mouth full of Danish, "well, yes, my sister's brother-in-law's daughter's friend had the same thing." Her head bobbed up and down, "Yes, yes. It definitely is gall bladder. Try some Pepto Bismal."

My desk faced the opposite wall of the tiny office that we shared which adjoined the patient waiting room. I had only been working as Dr. Papanos's nurse for the three months since returning to Connecticut and already I found myself feeling irritated much too often. The doctor, a balding, soft-spoken man in his mid-fifties, and Marjorie, his secretary with blonde, permed hair though in her early sixties, were both hypochondriacs. They usually spent the first hour of each morning comparing their respective ailments. He expressed his vague physical symptoms with an impotent whine; her woes sounded more like an assault. One of my jobs was to take their blood pressures each morning and afternoon and I swear they had an unspoken contest as to whose was the highest, the "winner" justifying the "Queen for a Day" kind of sympathy.

My attempts over that first month to have a relationship with Marjorie or the doctor were futile. I knew more about their physical functioning and orifices than I cared to and they knew nothing about me. Most of Marjorie's day was spent gossiping and giving advice to patients on the phone or to those who had come into the office. Though I was the nurse and we worked for a doctor, it seemed that Marjorie, who was bookkeeper and office manager, fancied herself the one with the medical knowledge. Probably osmosis. Most of my day was spent escorting patients into the examining room, doing blood and urine testing, running EKG's and, of course, paperwork. The pay was terrible, and there was no health insurance or other benefits. I really wanted to spend more time with the patients but Marjorie usually monopolized their time and if she found me talking with a patient, she would tell me that I needed to get back to my "work."

One of the many patients who presented herself at least once a week to see the doctor was a woman in her early twenties. Though we were the same age, Carol, Marjorie and Dr. Papanos seemed to be like peas in a pod. As soon as she arrived, she and Marjorie would "catch up" on that day's gossip and compare ailments.

I just smiled and said hello to Carol, then went back to my charting. Suddenly Carol gasped:

"Linda!" she exclaimed, coming over to my desk as Marjorie swiveled around in her chair, "The last thing I heard was that you had a positive pap smear! Is everything okay?"

I sat momentarily stunned. It was true, but this kind of information is personal and confidential! I was furious, but knew that if I showed it, Carol wouldn't tell me what I wanted to know. Forcing a smile I said, "Well, yes, but everything is fine, now. Thank you for being so concerned..." and then casually, "how did you know?"

Oh, well, my friend, Lisa, works at the hospital lab and she told me."

"Lisa? Do I know her?" I asked, knowing full well that I didn't. "What's her last name?"

"It's Lisa Ferguson. Do you know her? A petite blonde, about our age."

"No, no, I don't think I do. Well, thanks for your concern."

On my lunch break, I ran out to a pay phone and called the hospital lab. I asked to speak to the supervisor and told him how enraged I was that confidentiality had been violated. He insisted that Lisa was completely professional and would never do anything like that, but said he would "look into it." I never heard back from him.

One Friday afternoon, Marjorie sat at her desk with a cup of coffee and a chocolate-covered doughnut, as the little radio on top of the file cabinet droned the national news. She chewed and swallowed the first bite and washed it down with coffee, then said: "I don't understand why I can't lose weight, I hardly eat anything!"

I guess I had reached the breaking point. I was boiling and I thought: what do you mean you hardly ever eat? What the hell are you doing now? It's more like you hardly ever do anything BUT eat!

The next thing out of her mouth was a comment in response to a news story about a campus demonstration: "These young people today don't know anything. They are just trying to cause trouble and stir things up. They should learn to behave themselves!"

Whirring around in my chair I snapped, "And I suppose YOU know everything! YOU just have all the answers, don't you? Well, I've got news for you: You are just a close-minded, busy-body gossip. A meddlesome, quarrelsome, snoop!"

Her face was bright red and her startled eyes swam behind her glasses like fish in a bowl. She exploded from her chair and stormed into Dr. Papanos's office, slamming the door behind her.

Still trembling, I tried to go back to my paperwork, but couldn't concentrate. I had taken her manipulation and underhanded abuse far too long.

Not more than ten minutes later, Dr. Papanos called me into his office. Marjorie had passed me in the hallway and though her eyes were reddened and teary, she gave me a victorious glare.

"You've really upset Marjorie." he began, " She's crying and insists that if you continue to work here, she'll leave. I really need a bookkeeper, so I'm afraid I'll have to let you go. Is there anything you want to say?"

I told him what a shambles his filing and billing system was and that she wasn't doing the job she always boasted that she was doing. Trying to give him a picture of what she was really like, I told him about her gossiping and giving medical advice. He didn't want to hear it. She had him buffaloed. It was time for me to find another job, anyway. This one was far from what I'd hoped it would be and I knew that soon the right job would come along.

It's eleven o'clock, do you know where your R.N. is?

My next job was as an evening charge nurse at a pricey, "good" convalescent home in a wealthy town in Fairfield County, Connecticut. I learned quickly that the place was continually understaffed, poorly managed and often lacked even the basics for care like soap and clean bed linen. It was on one snowy evening that my relief for night staff called and said that she would be a "couple of hours" late and would I punch her card in at eleven. I told her that if I punched her in, I would have to punch out and I wouldn't get paid. "I'm not coming in, then." she said and hung up the phone. Infuriated, I called the director of nurses at home and told her what had happened.

"I'll look into it tomorrow." she yawned. New to the wonderful world of nursing homes, I didn't realize then that that kind of thing was an everyday occurrence. "In the meantime, you'll have to stay till the morning."

"I'm tired and I don't want to stay. I have plans for tomorrow and I need to sleep." I said, feeling a sinking, sick feeling in my stomach.

"A nurse has to be in the building at all times."

"A-wing's regular night nurse, Gail, is already here." I said.

"She's an LPN. By law there has to be an RN so if you don't stay, you'll be responsible for anything that happens," she threatened. "I'll be in as early as I can. See you in the morning." and she hung up the phone. I wish I had known that if I had refused, she would have had to come in.

After knocking softly on a confused patient's door, I walked over and stood at Martha's bedside, "It's Linda, the nurse, Martha, I have your medication." I said as I touched her shoulder.

She sat bolt upright in bed, white hair disheveled and though she had seen me many times, she said what she usually said, "Young man, what are you doing in my bedroom?"

"Martha, I'm Linda, your nurse."

"Oh no you're not!" she said indignantly before she launched into her trademark routine, "Help. Rape. PO-leeece! Help. Rape. PO-leece!" though she took her pills somewhere between saying "Rape" and "PO-leece". This would continue for perhaps a half an hour until she tired herself out and fell asleep.

After passing midnight medications and helping the nurse's aides get all of the patients' diapers changed and settled back to sleep, I sat down at the B-wing desk to do some charting. The aides had gone to take their break and all was quiet. It wasn't too long before I heard rumbling and spewing echoing from the darkened hallway in the direction of A-wing. It almost sounded like someone was in respiratory distress, or even a "death rattle." I moved quickly from behind the desk and saw a dark shadow in the middle of the hallway at the far end. As I walked closer, I realized that it was a large, reclined lounge chair with someone in it and when I stood within ten feet, there was Gail, covered with a blanket, mouth gaping in loud snores. She must have had a sinus condition, enlarged tonsils and adenoids, a cold, allergies or all of the above because I had never heard such sounds coming from a human before. I called her name loudly a few times before one of the aides from her wing came around the corner and told me not to bother.

"She won't wake up so don't even try." she smiled.

"Why?" I asked, "Does she do this every night?"

"She sure does. Smell her breath." the aide suggested.

I moved closer and got the distinct whiff of alcohol.

Moaning, I then whispered,"Does anyone know?"

"You mean like the Director of Nurses?"

"Yes."

"Oh, yeah, they know, but Gail's been here for years. Do you actually think anyone "upstairs" gives a damn whether someone actually cares for these patients? They just want warm bodies. Don't you know that profit is all that matters to them? Honey, you must be new to this kind of work, but don't worry, you'll learn," she laughed, "you'll learn."

"...You're going to die full!"

I quickly realized nursing homes weren't for me, so my next position was in a general hospital working as a staff nurse on a medical-surgical floor. Janice was the pear-shaped head nurse with bright red hair who was very knowledgeable and as efficient as a Sherman Tank. She always got the job done.

After report, all of the staff helped with setting up breakfast trays and feeding patients who were unable to help themselves.

"Open your mouth, Fred!" I yelled several times, but his blank eyes stared off into the yellowness of the hospital wall and he continued chewing mechanically, though there was nothing in his mouth. "Open up!" No response. I sighed. This poor man who was incontinent, and unable to do anything but eat, when fed, was a victim of a severe stroke. He was being transferred that afternoon to a nursing home where he could live for years like that – too many did. How ironic that he had ended up as he began life: in diapers, being fed pureed baby food. Was "saving lives" to live like a vegetable for years and years what it was all too often about? Occasionally I had considered not feeding patients like Fred – why perpetuate this kind of existence? It was no life. And what about those who loved him: they came to visit every day and talked to his blank face. And then, once in the convalescent home, after some time, the visits would be further and further apart, and then his family would only visit on his birthday or holidays and then sometimes not at all.

"Fred, open your mouth! I ordered, "Fred, do you hear me?" I pushed the spoonful of Gerber Peach Cobbler between his tight lips and his mouth snapped open suddenly. Quickly, I shoved the orange puree in, some running out both sides of his mouth. He bit down hard on the spoon, his teeth making a sickening cracking sound against the metal.

"Damn!" I whispered as I shuddered from the grating sound. I hoped he hadn't broken any teeth. Using both hands, I gently pinched his mouth open and was relieved to find that the teeth he did have were still intact.

Jill, the nurse's aide, was feeding Fred's roommate in the next bed. She was having the same struggle as I was except Albert, unlike Fred, was very verbally expressive.

"Aw, come on, Al, open up and have some breakfast!" Jill pleaded.

"NO!" he said, "I'm gonna die, Oh God, I'm gonna die!"

"You're not going to die now, Al. Please, now, open up and eat some breakfast."

Al continued repeatedly to insist, "I'm gonna die! Oh no, I'm gonna die. I'm gonna die, Oh God, I'm gonna die." Though Al had used those phrases over and over for the two weeks that he had been on Seven South, they didn't seem to have much meaning to him. Jill kept trying to reassure him that he wasn't dying with the hope that he might eat. Finally, after Al said "I'm gonna die" for the umpteenth time, Jill pinched his mouth open and shoved in a mouthful of food:

"Well, if you're going to die, you're going to die full!" she said. And the patient chewed and swallowed the food.

No Vacancy

While working as charge nurse on an evening shift, a female patient, in her late eighties, was found to have died quietly. The nurse's aide who had found her, was afraid of dead people and refused to go back into her room. After making the necessary calls, I went in to do the post-mortem care, though I never had before. The pasty coolness of her flesh, the open-eyed stare and gaping mouth made me uneasy and I found myself talking to the woman and myself, telling us both that this would be over soon. As with most medical "kits" the Shroud Kit came with instructions: 1) Thoroughly cleanse body. 2) Using gauze, tie mouth shut around top of head, after inserting dentures, if applicable. 3) Using gauze, secure wedding ring to finger using a figure-8 around wrist, as shown. 4) Using gauze, secure wrists together, as illustrated. 5) Using gauze, secure ankles together, as illustrated. 6) Secure ID tag to big toe. 7) With absorbent pad under buttocks, center body on shroud. 8) Wrap body in shroud and tie, as illustrated. 9) Secure ID tag to outside of shroud.

The funeral home would be by in the morning so I called the orderly to help me take the body down to the basement. The hospital morgue had three separate cooler drawers and when Lee and I arrived with the body, we found that all three were occupied. With much struggle and adjusting, we managed to maneuver the corpse into the middle cooler, on top of, and toe to head with the other body.

The next morning, I got a call from the Director of Nursing, a former nun. She was irate and told me in no uncertain terms that a female corpse must NEVER share the same slab with a male corpse!

Sitting down on the job

One morning, after helping with trays and "feeds," part of my assignment was to take the blood pressures of all of the thirty-two patients on the floor. Half way through the job, I entered a room where I found a patient crying. She was going in for a removal of a breast mass later that morning. I asked her if I could sit with her awhile and she nodded and smiled. Sitting on the side of bed, I took her hand, which she squeezed tightly.

"I'm so scared." she whispered, her eyes brimming with tears. Lisa was in her late thirties with two small children and had many questions about what was going to happen to her. We sat for sometime talking until she felt a little better, then I finished my blood pressures.

Just before lunch, Janice, the Head Nurse, called me into the nurse's lounge and closed the door. "It has come to my attention that you were not pulling your weight this morning. I understand that you were sitting and socializing with the patient in '702'."

I was stunned for a moment, not even considering reassuring a patient "socializing". Then I felt my face flush. "Janice! The poor woman was crying! Are you telling me that I should have grabbed her arm, taken her blood pressure and thrown a 'don't worry' over my shoulder as I left the room?"

"I'm telling you that a couple of minutes would have been sufficient. There's no need to get comfortable. I don't want to hear that you've been sitting down on the job again, unless it's your break time."

"Well, then," I said, trying to control my shaking, "Consider the time I spent with Mrs. Wallace my break time!" And I got up and left the room.

Not long after that, I found an ad in the paper for a long term care facility that wanted weekend nurses for twelve hour shifts. The pay was so high that I thought there had been a typo. When I called the Winslow Manor and was told that, indeed, the amount was correct, I promptly set up an appointment for an interview. Working there, I could make more in 24 hours than I was making in 40 at the hospital! Though I knew that I didn't like nursing home work, I certainly didn't like my job on Seven South either, so I decided working fewer hours for more money would make up for my growing frustration and distaste for my profession. It was probably at that moment that I admitted somewhere in the back folds of my conscious mind, that I didn't like being a nurse and that the system had licked me. But I rationalized that I was divorced then and had to support myself and daughter. This would give me more money and more time for myself and Meagan. On my last day working at the hospital, I met Dr. Papanos in the elevator. He was friendlier than he had ever been since he had fired me. Clearing his throat he said, "You know I had to let Marjorie go. I found that she had been spending most of her day on the phone. My bookkeeping and files were a disaster: there were accounts from years ago that had not even been billed!"

"I tried to tell you." I said, surprised that he would have even admitted what he had. "I really appreciate your telling me."

He shook his head, "She had been with me for so long and..." he coughed, "I hear you're leaving the hospital."

"Yes."

"Well, good luck." he smiled.

"Thanks."

Her own, personal fly swatter

Winslow Manor was, to say the least, a dump. It was dark, hot and rundown and smelled of urine, feces and filth. I was directed to the personal office "upstairs" and walked through a maze of corridors lined with white-haired wrinkled faces who reached for me with crooked fingers, wailed and laughed. A pretty nurse with dark hair noticed what must have been a horrified expression on my face. At that very moment I had been thinking about turning around and forgetting the whole thing, money and all.

"It's not that bad," she said, smiling.

Upstairs was air-conditioned, light and quiet. I met with the personnel director who told me that Winslow had just been bought by a very wealthy man who would be renovating the entire two-hundred bed facility. He wanted to make Winslow Manor a "showplace" of model patient care. The job was mine if I wanted it and would I be willing to do some occasional shifts as the nursing supervisor? Though I had never done supervisory work before, I assured her that I could. Why not? I knew I was a quick learner and besides, that meant even more in my paycheck.

Winslow's new owner, John Steinberg, was a short, round, bald man who was married with grandchildren but was constantly asking me and some of the other younger nurses out on dates. We all politely declined. He had the Manor painted and put up new curtains and wallpaper but the place was full of roaches and flies. Jo, one of the other supervisors, who had been there for many years, told me that they had just recently gotten screens for the windows.

"This is nothing," she said, smiling. "The fly population is much less now. Was a time, not long ago, when we'd gone in to do a dressing change on a necrotic bedsore and it would be full of maggots."

"Oh my God! Maggots? How disgusting!"

"Yeah, it was." she grinned, "But you know, they did a damn better job of debriding than any doctor I've known. Clean that dead tissue right out of there."

One Saturday, when I was working as supervisor, John called and told me that a Mr. and Mrs. Herbert would be stopping in for a tour of Winslow Manor. They were considering putting Mr. Herbert's elderly mother into a nursing home because she needed total care. "These people will be private pay so I want them to be impressed. We've got to get rid of all of these state cases. Give them a nice tour of the facility and I'll be in later."

Mr. and Mrs. Herbert arrived just after noon and I showed them around the place. I tried not to laugh when, each time I looked at them, they looked more and more distressed. Though the place had been painted and papered, I'm sure their experience was more horrifying than my first encounter with Winslow Manor, because they were considering placing a family member there. I would have felt awkward and uncomfortable if I hadn't found it so amusing. Here I was "giving a tour" of a place that had to pay me big bucks just to keep me and these poor people would have to pay to have their mother stay there. Several times they tried to gracefully leave, but I was having too much fun and sweetly insisted that they continue. They were too polite to refuse. The "tour" finale was back in my office for "questions and answers." Mr. and Mrs. Herbert, squirming in their seats across from my desk, briefly made small talk before I asked them about the prospective patient. At that same time, two flies, who had been buzzing and diving around the room, landed on the desk between us, one on top of the other. On a roll because this whole "tour" thing had been such a joke and the flies were the "icing on the cake," I couldn't stand it another minute. As the three of us stared at the two copulating flies, I cleared my throat.

"Of course," I began, in the best all-business tone I could muster under the circumstances, "of course, if your mother becomes one of our patients, she will be issued her own personal fly swatter." After which Mr. and Mrs. Herbert rose and promptly left.

Ten minutes later, John came into the office in his usual suit and tie, minus the jacket. He was mopping beads of sweat off of his balding head with a yellowish handkerchief. "Well?" he said excitedly, "were they here?"

"Oh yes," I smiled, "They were here alright."

"Well?"

"Well what?" I asked, wanting him to sweat some more.

"Well, did they like the place?"

"Like the place?" I said enthusiastically, "They said they'd never seen anything like it before."

Break times for staff were spent in our "staff dining room," an "L" in one of the hallways where ambulatory retarded or chronic psychiatric patients could come and either sit and watch us eat or beg for food. Irate family members could easily corner us there, too. There were soda and candy machines in the dining alcove. The soda machine was the kind with the cups that dropped down first, then ice, soda and syrup followed. Though I never ate or drank anything that I didn't bring from home, the rule amongst the staff was only buy Seven-Up from the soda machine. That way, if a roach happened to fall into the cup from inside the syrup shoot, you could see it in the clear soda and dump it out.

One lunch break, several of the nurses and I were eating salads that we had ordered from a nearby deli. Bessie, the sixty-four year old retarded woman who had been a patient at Winslow Manor for most of her life was sitting in the far corner, chin in her hands, watching us eat. She wore her usual pink floral dress, black cardigan and steel-toed work boots, her yellowish-white hair sticking out in all directions. Earlier, when I had been the first to arrive, I had found Bessie sitting in the "staff dining room" masturbating.

"Bessie," I had said firmly, "I've spoken to you before about that. You need to go to your room and close the door. That's something you do in private. It's time for you to leave, now, we're going to have our lunch."

"Please, Nurse, don't make me leave. I want to stay. I won't do that choo choo anymore. Promise. Buy me a candy bar?" she had asked with her toothless grin.

"Bessie," I had said, "if you sit quietly, down here away from the table and keep your hands out from under your dress, when we're done eating, I'll buy you a candy bar."

She grinned again. "I promise."

About half way through our lunchtime and its usual chatter about patients and complaints about administration absurdities, (though on weekends we rarely saw anyone from the "Ivory Tower") there was a lull in the conversation. Sitting quietly for a moment, I felt something small, like a pea, hit my head.

"Something just fell into my hair." I said to Vicky, the nurse beside me.

Peering through her glasses, she examined my head, then gasped, "Oh my God, there's a big roach in your hair!"

Repulsed I let out a yelp and flipped my head and hair forward. The roach was catapulted directly into the nurse's salad across the table from me. She let out a scream and slammed the lid of its Styrofoam container shut, then tossed the whole mess into the garbage can: "That's it! Now I'm really pissed! I've had it with this damn place!" and she got up and left. Momentarily shocked and silent, we then laughed and launched into further complaints and tirades about the place. It was the job we loved to hate. We all knew that everything was wrong but it felt too overwhelmingly absurd. We just laughed it off.

Once in awhile, John would agree to have the place fumigated but of course, didn't want to spend too much, so he hired some fly-by-night exterminators. The day they were to spray, patients were moved and each wing, in turn, was "sealed off" and fumigated. They waited several hours, then patients were shuffled around again until the entire facility had been covered. Though the wings had been sealed off I smelled the pesticides as they seeped out. It was after that that I began having irregular heartbeats from time to time and though the cardiologist said that it was "stress" I believe that exposure to toxins play a big part in many maladies. What further convinced me was that within the week following that fumigation, four patients with respiratory diagnoses died.

"She's an old woman..."

Long-term care facilities have a doctor who serves as a medical director. He or she oversees the care that is provided by doctors who have patients there and he usually attends to patients in the facility as well. There is no doctor in residence, or readily available all of the time, as there is in hospitals, so when a patient needs a doctor's attention, the nurse or nursing supervisor has to call for one. Since a long-term care facility does not have the set-up for acute situations, when necessary, patients are sent to the hospital emergency room. Winslow Manor's medical director was an Arabic doctor who had somehow managed to accumulate a good three-quarters of the two-hundred patients in residence there. He rarely laid eyes on his patients, let alone examine them. An annual physical exam is required by the state and so, Dr. Shimed would come in, fill out the physical exam form when each patient's would come due and charge the state or Medicare a hefty fee.

One evening when I was working a floor, I found a patient in acute respiratory distress. After checking her vital signs, making her as comfortable as possible and asking a nurse's aide to sit with her, I went out to the desk to call Dr. Shimed.

"Yes, Linda, what is it?" he asked with a sigh.

"It's Irene Barton." I said, " She has a temperature of 102, her respirations are 42 and pulse 130. Her lungs are very congested."

"Linda," he sighed again, "what would you like me to do? She's an old woman."

"Doctor, she has a fever. She probably has pneumonia. I would like to send her to the hospital for chest x-rays and antibiotics."

"She's an old woman." he repeated.

"I'm going to quote you on that when I write my note in her chart," I said as I noticed her age in the kardex on the desk in front of me. I remembered that Dr. Shimed had recently told me he turned sixty-five and was "in the best shape he'd been in in his life" because he was now using a treadmill. "She's seventy," I added, "five years older than you..." but he had already hung up the phone.

Not more than sixty seconds later, Dr. Shimed called back: "Linda," he said, all business, "Send Irene to the E.R."

Chapter 6

Running On Empty

Alton Manor was a small, private nursing home with twenty-two beds downstairs and fourteen up: most of the geriatric patients were confused, incontinent and had to be fed; many were combative, some wandered. On nights, one nurse and two nurse's aides would cover both floors, but tonight there had been only myself and one aide. After Vi and I had done last rounds, changing urine-soaked diapers on most of the patients, cleaning one who had smeared feces on himself, the bed rails and wall behind his bed, I gave medications. Most of the pills had to be crushed then mixed in applesauce then forced between clenched teeth. Sometimes the mixture would be spewed back out at me, so I had to be quick.

It was six-thirty a.m. and I felt the expected nausea. After working a night shift, my system was always upset enough to make me queasy for the next several days. When the scheduled night nurse had called in sick the night before, I had just finished working an evening shift, and though I tried to find a replacement for the night nurse from the on-call list, nobody was available. I decided to do a double shift and stay on until morning. Why not? I was already there, could use the money and would save the director of nursing from having to come in and cover.

For about five years, I had been working with Dun's Nursing Care Agency which was like an "office temp" agency for nurses instead of office staff. Jobs varied from doing staff relief in hospitals, intensive care units, and nursing homes to an occasional home case, and I found it better than being in the same place all of the time. I could get in, do my job, and get out, which made it easier to avoid politics and gossip. It was tolerable at best, but I had become more aware that I hated what nursing had become for me and what I had become because of it. I was a single parent and though the agency paid the best, I had to take last minute shifts that became available, mostly evenings, nights, holidays and weekends. I would get home just in time to let my baby-sitter go off to work and to get Meagan, my seven-year old daughter breakfast and off to school.

I wondered how anyone could do permanent night shifts, though those who did told me that one could get used to them. Some even liked nights better and I could understand why. On nights at Alton Manor and in the hospitals where I had worked, we only had to care for the patients; rarely were there families, doctors or administrators around. Day shifts were fast-paced and crazy with management and owners prowling around and mandatory meetings that accomplished little besides putting us behind in our patient care and paperwork. Evenings were the time when the patients' families visited. Feeling guilty about having their parents in a nursing home, they were often angry about the lack of care and were full of complaints, demands and threats. No matter where I worked, all shifts were understaffed: administration always blamed that on we nurses calling in sick, but it really came down to dollars and cents – they didn't want to have to pay more staff or overtime.

Coming to the end of a sixteen hour shift, I had finished doing treatments and final charting then I sank down in the plastic upholstered chair in the empty day room. The T.V. was tuned to "Morning Stretch" with a trim, blonde Barbie doll of a woman chirping, "OOOOooooo now doesn't this feel sooooo good!?"

"No!" I growled back at her. I was shaky inside. I thought about eating something just to keep my eyes open this last half hour until my seven a.m. relief came, but my queasiness made me decide to wait. I had snacked often during the night while doing paperwork not because I was hungry but to stay awake.

The next thing I knew, Sue, Alton Manor's Director of Nursing, was shaking my shoulder. It was six forty-five. Momentarily disoriented, I stammered a "good morning" and an explanation that I had just sat down and had been working a double shift. She didn't say much except that it could happen to anyone. In fact, she reassured me, it had once even happened to her.

I went home and early in the afternoon, after three hours of sleep, I got out of bed. The nausea persisted, but I made a cup of tea and some dry toast and forced them down anyway. I still was shaky. When the phone rang, it was Becky from Dun's Nursing Care saying that she had gotten a complaint from Sue at Alton Manor: I had been sleeping on the job.

"That ungrateful bitch." I said to Becky, "See if I stay again and help her out. Next time, I'll call her and she can come in to work!"

Becky, who was a master at handling people, agreed that I had done Sue a favor and that she was indeed ungrateful. "Don't worry about this," she said, "it's no big deal and I know you're a good nurse. It's happened to all of us at one time or another. Sleeping is the least of our problems, it could've been worse."

It was after the Alton Manor incident that I felt some uneasiness. It momentarily occurred to me that I was in a system where everyone, patients as well as healthcare professionals were victims. It seemed that no matter what I did, it was never good enough and that I could and should have done more. Nothing ever seemed to get done with the patient and paperwork overload. It always felt incomplete: too often minimal care was all that could be hoped for and short cuts had to be taken. There was rarely the satisfaction of a "job well done," but rather frustration. Still, nurses aren't allowed to be human, there wasn't time. The fast pace and high stress of a busy med-surg floor, emergency room or intensive care unit could push anyone to their limits. Unlike most professions where mistakes are correctable, or at least not life-threatening, in healthcare, human error is inexcusable.

But those big mistakes only happened to other people. By comparison, mine were small and inconsequential.

For the next three months, I continued as I had been for the previous five years, working for the Critical Nursing Agency in intensive care and coronary care units, nursing homes, emergency rooms and on oncology and medical-surgical floors in general hospitals. Working all shifts, fifty to sixty hours a week, I continued to do double shifts and "turnarounds" from an evening shift, up at six in the morning after four hours sleep, to work a day shift. Coffee and high sugar foods were my mainstay. In between working and caring for my daughter, I trained for running in races, took a class at a local college and was writing a novel. It felt good, like a high: helping people in my job, single parent, runner, student and writer. I was doing "it all" and felt fully in control, needed and important. The patients were a blur of respirators, Foley bags, IVs, nauseating odors, diagnosis, paperwork and demands. My focus was on the exhilaration, like the "thrill" of a high-speed chase or a crises-driven roller coaster ride. It was like walking on a tight rope. Except for a rare reprimand, which I easily shrugged off as coming from an "ungrateful bitch," I belonged to the big powerful machine that stood for healing, care, and compassion.

One night I awoke from a sound sleep in a cold sweat. My heart was pounding so fast that I felt it would pulsate right out of my throat. I could barely breathe and I felt as if I was having a heart attack. Struggling for air, I got up out of bed but was so dizzy that I had to be sick. After crawling to the bathroom and vomiting, I lay flat on the floor, held perfectly still so the room wouldn't spin, groped for and found the phone and dialed "911." When the EMTs arrived, they called a neighbor to come and stay with Meagan, but she had already awakened and stood crying, "Mommy! Mommy!" as I was carried out to the ambulance. I had become the patient.

"I'm okay, Meagan, Mommy's okay," I said to reassure her and myself.

In the emergency room my heart rate dropped from 120 to 50 beats per minute. Feeling cold and alone, it seemed that everyone was busy with other patients and more important matters. When an intern finally examined me and my EKG strip, he wisely asked me about my life:

how many hours did I work and how did I relax and take care of myself on my days off? He said that my EKG looked good and after we had talked for a few minutes he said, "It looks like you're burning the candle at both ends. Something has got to give and it's going to be your health if you continue at this pace."

All of my other tests were negative and I was discharged from the hospital early the next day. After taking the week off to reflect on my life as honestly as I could, I decided to leave nursing for awhile. In spite of the years of education and experience, something was very wrong. How had I gotten to this point? Where had my dreams gone and what had happened to the compassionate young woman who, after coming out of nursing school fifteen years earlier, had sincerely believed she could help people? How did I really feel about myself as a nurse, my colleagues and the modern healthcare system? Were we really helping people? I needed some time to sort things out...

I was ashamed to admit I was a nurse

Two years later, I was sitting in the elegant lobby of the Grand Hyatt Hotel, momentarily watching people go by and listening to the piano music weave throughout the muffled roar of New York City, when I noticed a woman heading directly toward me. She looked at me as if she knew me and because I didn't know her, I glanced to my right and my left but there was no one else near. The woman was well-dressed in a tailored navy suit and carrying a brief case. She plopped down right next to me and yanking off her right shoe, rubbed her foot with a sigh as she lifted it across her knee:

"Look at this red bump here on my foot," she said to me. "It really hurts. I've had it for several months now, what do you think I should do?"

After asking her a few questions and affirming that it must really hurt, I suggested that she see a podiatrist. She thanked me, put on her shoe and walked painfully away.

Amused, I wondered why she had chosen me out of the others in the lobby and questioned her sanity for asking a total stranger for medical advice and my sanity for answering her. Having been a nurse for so many years, I thought perhaps I had an "R.N." tattooed on my forehead that I was unaware of. I had left nursing burned out and disillusioned, hating what my profession had become for me and what I had become because of it.

For most of my years as a nurse, except for a short time in nursing school, my career as a "Florence Nightingale" was not what I thought it would be. What had happened to the loving, caring person that I was? How had that woman with great visions of helping people become so cynical? When I was practicing nursing, I had made it a point not to tell people what I did for a living, believing that this would save me from having to listen to someone's medical history and complaints. The fact was I had lost so much respect for myself in my profession and in mainstream medicine as a whole, that I was ashamed to admit I was a nurse.

With only a few exceptions, the feelings I have about those years I spent as a registered nurse are those of revulsion, inadequacy and shame. Though my colleagues, employers and patients would tell you that I was "good nurse" and some would even say a "supernurse," something was missing for me. Always smiling and playing the role, I did what I thought was expected of me, but I felt empty and ineffective at most of the jobs that I had, from doctor's offices and clinics to ER's, ICU's and nursing supervisor positions. Though never showing it, nor admitting it to myself, I went to work each day with dread.

When my love-hate relationship with "modern medicine" culminated in burnout, I was very angry and blamed the system for not allowing me to be the loving, caring person and nurse that I knew I was. The true reason was that I didn't know how. I couldn't give what I didn't have and the bunk that I was taught in nursing school about "professional distance" was a good reason to not look at my own fear of getting close. Being a "victim" of the big business modern medicine machine, I honestly believed, as most of us do, that when you were a nurse or a doctor, you absolutely had to keep a "professional distance" to protect yourself. You could not show emotion and you had to keep your head and so, you could not open your heart. Indeed, it's a fine line, but let me clarify something. When I say "expressing emotion," I'm not talking about inappropriate outbursts of hysteria that cloud thinking and logic. I don't mean that we become so involved with every patient that we take them all home with us (even though there are some I may want to take home with me.) Opening our hearts doesn't necessarily mean that we have to do something. We can often be the most effective when we can just be.

I had gotten caught up in the modern medicine machine and "burned out." It was easy to blame being stressed out on the medical system because nurses like to complain amongst themselves so I always had an appreciative audience as well as plenty of encouragement and group participation. I loved being the martyr, it was the only way I knew to justify my existence and I was willing to die to prove it. Then came that night when I became the patient...

Over the next two years, I began to finally take responsibility for my own behavior and stopped blaming others and the system and rediscovered my own heart of healing. It was during that time that I began a relationship with someone I had never known – myself.

We cannot do great things, only
small things with great love.
—Mother Teresa

PART THREE

transition... learning to touch and be touched

CHAPTER 7

I USED TO BE NEARLY PERFECT (BUT THEN I GOT BETTER!)

Until ten years ago I was nearly perfect. I was ever competent, intelligent, composed, in control of myself and emotions, sensitive, assertive and kind and gentle at all times. Most certainly I was non-judgmental of others and was a good mother, wife, friend and "super-nurse." Those occasional emotional outbursts of tears or rage were because of something someone else did or said, or some other event or circumstance in my life. Those little doubts about my near perfection were just in my imagination and not reality. At that time, I was in a second marriage with a difficult man (my first husband had been difficult, too) and had convinced my husband to go to couples' therapy. I told him that we needed help but knew that *he* was the one that *really* needed the help.

In spite of my perfection, I somehow found myself at a weekend workshop for Adult Children of Alcoholics where I came face to face with one of my "demons." It exploded from my upper chest, shoulders and down my arm into my right fist that was clenched full of crayons for an experiential exercise that we were doing. It stabbed the crayons wildly at a piece of paper. It roared from my belly in alien screams and, the crayons hurled aside, bloodied my fists against the rough carpet. As four therapists physically subdued me, they threw a pillow under my pounding fists.

"Hit the pillow," one of them urged, "or you'll hurt yourself."

My fist bashed the pillow aside and, with distant disbelief, I heard my "demon" hiss, "I WANT to hurt myself!"

This unfamiliar rage I called my "demon," curled back inside of me like a tidal wave, leaving me exhausted and held helplessly to the floor, its screams becoming my gasps, its red eyes disappearing into my blurred vision and tears.

Returning from the weekend, feeling like I had been skinned alive, I called my therapist from the pay phone at the Grand Union, after taking my daughter to school.

"I need to see you," I whispered.

"There's a cancellation at two o'clock this afternoon."

"Nothing sooner?"

"No, sorry."

"I hope I make it till then."

"That bad?"

"I can't talk. I'll see you at two."

"Hang in there."

I don't remember ever feeling so badly in all of my life and was sure that I would die at any moment.

Those feelings of rage, grief and fear that I had labeled unacceptable and had, up until that fateful weekend, kept buried in my unconscious, were now overwhelming. I started going to Adult Children of Alcoholics twelve-step meetings and, sure that I was crazy, now found comfort in the company of others who seemed to feel the same. It was not new to me that "Daddy had a drinking problem." What was new was the realization that it had affected me so deeply and completely. There had been incidents that I had not remembered at all until I started to explore my feelings.

Arriving at a conference in San Francisco, and realizing that I had several hours before I could check into my room, I went downstairs to the exhibit area. Among the exhibitors was a booth for something called Rosen Method Bodywork with photographs that looked like people were getting a massage. Having been on the plane for hours, their offer of a "free fifteen minute mini-demonstration" was appealing. I noticed, then, that my body was stiff and my neck ached. "Boy," I thought, "I sure could use a massage."

I was led behind a curtained partition. I lay face-down on a massage table, and a gentle, white haired woman in her mid fifties asked me if I had any pain in my body. I told her that I very often had neck and shoulder pain.

"When did you first have this neck and shoulder pain?" she asked me as she placed her hands quietly on my neck. She didn't move her hands much and I remember thinking, before I answered her, that this wasn't like any massage I had ever had.

"I must have been about ten years old," I answered, thinking about the terrible neck pain I had then when I borrowed my best friend's Mom's soft neck brace that helped to support my head.

"And what was going on in your life at that time?"

I thought for a moment, feeling her warm hands on my neck that felt like steel. Why had I borrowed Debbie's Mom's cervical collar instead of asking my own parents for help? "Well," I replied, "Mom had just had her first cancer surgery and Dad was drinking again..."

"And what was that like for you as a ten year old?"

Before I could even reply, years and years of overwhelming, unidentifiable feelings exploded through me with such intensity that I began to sob and I continued to sob until she told me that our time was up.

So there I was again, feeling alone, vulnerable and exposed. It was still too early to check into my room so I went into a stall in the Ladies

Room, shut the door and cried. Though a part of me was afraid that the tears would never stop, another part of me intuitively knew that it was time to let them flow. Somehow this gentle woman had opened me up so that I had experienced those feelings that I had had almost thirty years earlier as a little girl. It had been terrifying but somehow wonderful. I knew on a gut level that this was good for me – that this is what I needed to heal. I was scared, exhilarated and intrigued – I had to know more!

The next day, I booked a private one hour session and found the experience very different from the day before but again both painful and wonderful at the same time. I could not contain my curiosity: I had had a glimpse of who I really was somewhere under the rage and pain and I promised myself I would continue on this path.

Back on the East Coast, I started going to a Rosen Practitioner in New York City every week. Melissa was a gentle soul who was expecting her first child when we met. She had been a dancer, become anorexic and, through the hands-on work, no longer had an eating disorder. Our work together was one of the most powerful first steps for me on my journey.

I returned to California that summer for an intensive training. As it should be for all training in the healing arts, my training in the Rosen Method focused on my healing as well as the healing of those that I worked on. In all relationships we are both teacher and student.

At one particular day-long seminar in New York City, there had been a prospective student who had been particularly irritating to me. Though she was a woman in her early forties, she was in constant motion, like a hyperactive child. Leslie would go from sitting in her chair, both feet on the floor to loudly sighing and noisily crossing and uncrossing first one leg then the other, drawing nearly everyone's attention to her while the instructor was talking. Then she would sit cross-legged, Indian style, balancing precariously in her metal folding chair for a minute or two before stomping her feet back onto the floor. Frequently, Leslie would interject an off-the-wall comment or launch into a lengthy personal experience that was unrelated to the subject being discussed. Several times, though, the instructor had tactfully asked her to condense what she was saying and get to the point, Leslie became quite belligerent and defensive. I decided that she was a know-it-all, totally self-absorbed, self-righteous and insensitive to others. There was a roughness about her, a carelessness in the way she moved and she had a high-pitched, grating voice. I stayed as far away from her as possible, though the more I tried to avoid her during the morning, each time I looked around, she was there. Leslie was like a cat: when they know you don't like them, they climb on your lap.

One of the methods of teaching Rosen Method was to break the class into small groups of about six or seven and choose one student to be the patient while the instructor demonstrated and the rest of the group observed. When we were about to divide into our groups, I again moved away from Leslie. We counted off one to four and I got the number "four" group. So did Leslie.

I would venture to say that everyone in the group wanted to be chosen to be the one to be demonstrated on, especially me. My experiences with the Rosen sessions had been so revealing and powerful that I wanted every opportunity to get worked on. We were all there to learn to heal and be healed.

Sara, the instructor, looked from one to the other of those of us in group number four, "Who would like to be worked on?" she asked. We all raised our hands graciously but Leslie waved wildly, causing a commotion. Sara glanced at her and seemed annoyed. "Good," I thought, "at least she won't choose her." At that point, I didn't really care if she chose me, just as long as she didn't demonstrate on Leslie. I had heard enough of her ridiculous comments and annoying voice and would hate to see her take any more time and attention than she had already so far today.

I noticed Sara's eyes were on me and she was smiling. "Oh, good," I thought, "it looks like she's thinking about asking me to get on the table." Then Sara sighed softly, shifted her gaze toward Leslie and asked her if she wanted to be worked on.

I felt my anger rising up from my neck and throat. Hadn't Leslie, with all of her noise and distractions, gotten enough attention today? I was angry at Leslie and Sara and the injustice of it all! It didn't get any better, either. Leslie lay on the table and as Sara began the hands-on session, Leslie talked almost incessantly, body rigid and guarded, about superficial garbage. Totally disinterested, and angry, I took a bathroom break, just to get away for a time. When I returned, the session was going just about the same as when I left. Sara had tried many times to bring Leslie's focus into the present, into her body and into the feelings she may be experiencing. Leslie continued to talk loudly and non-stop.

"Can you feel how tight and guarded your body is?" Sara asked her quietly.

"Of course I can! I'm not stupid, you know!"

"I never thought that you were. Do you think you are?"

"You don't have to insult me!" Leslie growled.

"You seem angry." Sara observed.

"Hell, yes I am. I don't like being called stupid!"

Sara, continuing to keep her hands in gentle contact with Leslie's rock-hard upper back and shoulders, closed her eyes momentarily, then said, "Earlier today, you were doing an exchange with another student and I remember you saying that you were a very tender person. Is that what you are protecting here under the 'armor' of your back and shoulders?"

For a moment, there was silence and my attention, from somewhere out in space, immediately snapped back to the moment and Leslie. Something had changed dramatically. I could see Sara's hands rising and falling more quickly as they stayed in contact with Leslie's body. Then there was a shudder, some sighs, then Leslie began to sob. Tears filled my eyes and spilled down my cheeks. Leslie had softened, dropped her facade and become vulnerable, tender and real before my eyes and my feelings for her had turned to love.

"Daddy, stop!"

It was during Rosen Method intensives that I encountered many painful childhood memories, one of them being that I had been a victim of drunken, incestuous behavior. Several years before that, my therapist had asked me bluntly at the end of a session one day, if my father had ever sexually abused me. Indignant and shocked that she would ever think such a thing possible, I told her just that. She immediately apologized profusely but not before interjecting that my family dynamics were so "textbook." She had said, "You know, alcoholic father, sick mother..." I had brushed it off as an overzealous therapist and there it had stayed until I had the memory with the Touch that I could not deny. I had to be with the pain.

During a Rosen instructor's demonstration, where I was the patient and a small group of other students watched, I had an experience that changed my life. The instructor's hands were on my shoulders as I lay face down on the table with my eyes closed, and it felt as if she were pushing me very hard and I told her so.

"I'm just in gentle contact with your shoulders." Jean replied.

I continued to feel like I was being treated roughly and as I felt my anger rising into my throat, remembered that my Dad used to take my shoulders and jerk them back harshly. At the same time his big hands were clumsily pulling my shoulders back he'd remind me to "stand up straight". It used to irritate me but I never dared to say anything.

Jean continued to keep contact with my shoulders, as she gently pushed and pulled, though it felt more and more like an assault. I started to say something, but it came out as just a noise.

"What did you say?" Jean asked.

"Nothing." I replied, bewildered. What I had wanted to say seemed to have come out of nowhere and for some reason, my anger had turned to fear. Then a memory rose around me and enveloped me like a damp fog: shivering, I found myself to be about seven years old and almost asleep in my bedroom of the house I grew up in. Dad had just come into the room and was pulling and pushing my shoulders and I held my breath, pretending to be asleep. He had that terrible smell he always had when he acted mean and unpredictable – at seven I didn't realize that he had the smell of alcohol on his breath. It even would seep out of his pores.

"You started to say something," she persisted, "what was it?"

"I wanted to say, Daddy stop." I whispered.

"I didn't hear what you said."

"Daddy stop!" I said, my voice startling me so that my body jumped, my heart pounded in my throat and I felt short of breath.

"What's that about?" Jean asked. After I caught my breath, I told her about the memory of Dad in my bedroom. I could feel her silent but loving presence and those of my fellow students nearby.

A little later on in that same session, I was lying on my back and Jean had her hands on my jaw, another area that had always been tense and tight for me. As her fingers pressed into my jaw on both sides at the same time, I thought about how I used to put the bit into my pony's mouth. By squeezing either side of the back of her jaw and forcing her mouth open, I could easily slip the bit in and the bridle on.

When Jean asked me what I was noticing, I told her what I had just been thinking about. "Your jaw area has just gotten very tight," she observed, "much more than before and you're breathing seems very shallow and rapid, like you might be afraid."

As she spoke, I focused on my body. She was right, my jaw was so tight that it hurt and I was taking little gasps of air. Suddenly, I felt like I had been hit head-on by a truck: my mouth was forced open and something jammed inside almost totally blocking my breathing. At the same moment a huge weight crushed my chest and though I tried to fight just to get a breath, I was pinned fast so that I could only flail my legs uselessly for a moment and then became paralyzed. Hot tears squeezed from the sides of my eyes, I could make no sounds with my voice but my heart beat so loudly that it shook the room and there was a buzzing in my ears. I couldn't tell whether my eyes were opened or closed but everything was black except for flashes of silver-gray light. And though my nostrils burned with the stench of alcohol and my mouth was hot and salty I began to try to make sounds.

"Linda, what's happening?" Jean said, though she sounded like she was very far away. "What do you want to say?"

"I want to say Daddy, stop." I thought I heard myself say, but I hadn't.

"Say it, Linda" Jean gently encouraged, "say it, you're safe here."

Though in that moment, I felt that I was safe, the memory had been so real it was dizzying and I felt light-headed and nauseated. Then a wave of shame washed over me and the child's voice in my head said, "Daddy would never do that, he loves you." And then the voice repeated it several more times, my mother's voice joining in until I heard my own voice say out loud, "Daddy would never do that, he loves me. I was wrong, it wasn't Daddy, I made it all up."

"You made it all up?" Jean repeated, though I knew she didn't believe me.

"I was wrong, I lied," came out with my sobs, because that was as much of the truth as I could bear at that time. That 'secret' that had been locked up completely and securely in my unconscious, relentlessly guarded by my body, the sentry, had finally been unearthed. Though at that moment I was insisting that I had lied, I knew, as did those witnesses, that my 'secret' was no longer a 'secret' and in the telling, it had lost some of its power. What remained was an excruciating pain that I felt would kill me, but this was to be the beginning of a healing for me.

My sobbing pounded my body like an angry sea for what seemed like years but was probably moments or minutes. When the waves curled back into themselves, I felt like I had been beaten by them before they had flung me naked and raw onto a rocky beach. When I opened my eyes, Jean and the small group of students stood around me, all had tears in their eyes and on their cheeks. Two of the students were crying openly.

"What do you need from us?" Jean asked softly.

Without hesitation I said, "I need to be rocked."

Immediately, I was surrounded, enveloped and rocked by many loving arms all at the same time and in that place of warmth, acceptance and love, I cried my first tears of joy.

For many years, when I believed that I was nearly perfect, when I allowed myself a momentary experience of feeling, I felt completely insane. Who would want to closely examine the insanity of the life that I had created? Not me! Yes, I got up every morning, (with much dread) showered and brushed my teeth, convinced myself and everyone else that I was happy (damnit) and knew what I was doing in my job (I'd better be, what else could I possibly be qualified to do?) and in my relationships (weren't marriage and "romantic" relationships supposed to be miserable hard work?). I made a living, financially supported myself and my daughter (though had no clue how to nurture either of us) and paid my taxes. But the lifestyle I was living then did cause me to hurt myself physically and on some occasions, I went into a rage and hit my daughter and, when I was married, my step-son. I shudder to think of the emotional, psychological and spiritual trauma that I inflicted on those closest to me. At that time, my life was war and every day was a fight to survive, with "public enemy number one" being myself.

At first I was full of rage and angry at all of those people, places and things out there that were, as I saw it, the cause of all my problems. Then I was enraged and angry at myself because I should be able to control all of those people, places and things! What really made me angry, though, was when, through Touch, I started feeling vulnerable, needy and in pain! I couldn't want or need anybody! I couldn't be afraid, I had to know what to do, I had to know how to take care of everyone else! I had to be tough, strong! Tears were weak, rage was strong!

Through private sessions, my training in Rosen Method and other hands-on disciplines and attending twelve-step support groups and workshops, I gradually learned to "be" with myself and my feelings of rage, pain and fear. The neck and shoulder pain that I had experienced since childhood that was either excruciating spasms or feeling heavy and numb, like chunks of hard wood in those areas, began to lessen and I started to feel more and more alive.

Little by little I learned that strength lies in tenderness and anger is actually fear. Among the most profound revelations in my journey this far, was how difficult it was for me to admit that I loved my father! I was actually enraged at myself for loving him because he had been so abusive. It was around this time that Marion Rosen once said that "It's okay to love the bastard." Though I could never accept or condone his abusive behavior, I loved my father. Today, I have great empathy for those feelings he had that seemed to drag him around, making his life war. The feelings we have are the same, what we choose to do with them is our responsibility and choice.

Beginning with self love, we are finally able to love those in our lives and that love spills over into a universal love, a love of Love and a love of Life. It is always okay to love, in fact, all that we do is "love seeking to know itself..."

The little girl in the blue dress

Once, while doing hands-on work on a woman at a Rosen Intensive, I encountered my first validation of intuition that I could not ignore. Of course, since childhood I had been aware of my intuition but had not given it much credibility. My upbringing had not fostered self-trust.

Helga was a quiet, reserved woman from Germany who was tall and wore glasses. She sat silently at meals and I had never spoken with her until one day, during the intensive, when we were to work on each other. With her lying on the table and my hands on her painful, tight shoulders, I kept visualizing a little blonde girl, about three years old, in a blue dress playing in a garden singing joyfully. Each time I would visualize that, I'd just brush it away because it didn't fit with what Helga was saying. Finally after seeing the little girl in the garden for the fourth time, I decided to mention it to Helga. When I did, she began to sob but insisted that that was NOT her.

"Then why are you crying?" I asked.

And she cried loudly, "Because I wished I could be that little girl singing in the garden! My parents always punished me when I made any noise at all."

I was amazed at how right my intuition was and glad that I had made my vision known, because it had helped Helga as well as me. But my intuition was doubly affirmed when later that afternoon, Helga approached me to talk, "I didn't want to say anything earlier because it really frightened me that you would know, being that we've never met. But it's about the blue dress that you told me the little girl was wearing. You see, my mother only dressed me in blue. I was never allowed to choose any of my clothes – they all were blue. To this day, I hate the color blue and don't own anything that color." Wow! I was completely thrilled and excited that I had trusted my intuition enough to "put it out there."

As I continued with the bodywork sessions with Melissa in New York City, I was overjoyed to find that not only was I learning to know, trust and love myself, but little by little, the pain in my neck and shoulders lessened, then disappeared.

Fascinated with touch, I explored Reike, Shiatsu, Swedish Massage, Polarity and Bioenergetics (a releasing breathing technique) as well as continuing with more Rosen trainings. I started meditating and practicing Yoga every day and continued going to self-help groups as well as attending workshops and seminars. I would say that I had become so completely focused on my own healing, that it was often an obsession. I was very much in touch with that rage "demon" that I had encountered on that fateful weekend workshop, and much of my rage and anger at that time, was directed at my father.

I learned that anger and sadness belongs in the present. If it's rage and grief that I'm feeling, it's old anger and sadness that has been stored away in the unconscious mind and body for years and years. Something that I was aware of, but never gave a second thought to was that as long as I could remember, I would always cry uncontrollably at sad movies and stories or over other people's pain, but never would I be aware of my own sadness. Little transgressions of others could set me off into a rage and I had no idea how I could be so upset over such silly things. Of course, global injustice made me crazy, but I could never be in touch with, nor appropriately express anger or irritation in my everyday life. But now, I would go to my meetings and spew rage and grief at the God of my childhood and the universe and no one in particular and I was reminded of the woman on the psychiatric ward screaming and pounding her head into the concrete pillar so many years before. Then, I had thought it was her pain that had touched me so deeply, but I had become aware that it was my own pain she had touched.

Once during another Rosen training, I had asked Marion Rosen if it was alright to cry when you were working on a client.

"It's okay to cry," she said with a grin, "but don't drip on the client."

You might think that all of this self knowledge and healing stuff sounds painful and at times, it is. But it's well worth it! Something else that Marion said was that we can't selectively feel only the "good" feelings and not the bad. Either we're feeling or we're not.

Though at first I thought I WAS my feelings, I know now that I have feelings but I'm not my feelings. For years I felt I was nothing but bottled up feelings that I thought were "bad," making me a "bad" person. I didn't dare own them or acknowledge their existence to myself, let alone anyone else.

Another great bit of insight that I heard at a conference one time that has helped me and many of my patients was that "depression is anger that we don't feel we have a right to have." We do have a right to be angry, we have a right to have all of our feelings and to express them safely and appropriately! My mother once confided in me a year before she died that she thought cancer was anger turned inward. She would have known.

What I know now is that when I feel, I am alive. Feelings are not good or bad, they just are. Pain is a feeling and it is neither good nor bad, it just is. I can't live and love if I don't allow myself to feel. Only Dr. Spock, Vulcans and robots don't feel, humans feel. Humans have a body, mind and spirit which are all connected to and flow into one another. We cannot separate and treat only the body, only the mind or only the spirit. Healing has to include all three.

My life and love began when I was able to admit that I was a human being. This was a big step for me. On an unconscious level, I truly believed that I had to be perfect (it felt like a matter of life and death). Intellectually I knew that this was ridiculous and impossible but my deep feelings of shame and rage were certainly, in part, because I was imperfect and thus believed that I was undeserving and a failure. However, my life had been spent pretending that I was perfect and convincing the world (and hopefully myself) that I was the perfect nurse, mother and woman. If only the world and others would live up to my standards! If my frenzied life then had not been so pathetic and yes, so painful, I think that now I would be embarrassed by my arrogance. I wouldn't recommend being nearly perfect. It sounds absurd intellectually, most everyone would agree, but through my own experiences and those told to me by my friends, colleagues, patients and clients, too many of us who are stressed out and "burned out" are striving for perfection. Think of it! If I'm nearly perfect, no one is good enough. I can't love them and they can't love me! (Because I'm always right, even if I don't verbally express it.) Being perfect is too much work and in reality, life is good, simple and easy if we let it. It was in that moment when I finally accepted my human limitations that I became completely open to the limitlessness of Love.

I chose nursing as my career for many reasons, I am sure, but the one reason that looms out at me right now is that there was a part of that "nearly perfect me" that was sure that if I did it right and learned enough and was perfect at it, I COULD SAVE PEOPLE! I COULD FIX PEOPLE! This was unconscious in a very infantile place born out of fear and desperation: If I could save Mom from cancer and Dad from drinking, I could save me. I could be important, I could be the hero, my life would matter, I would matter!

Well, it was quite a relief when it finally struck the thick skull that I had, for years, been banging against my self-created concrete pillar, that I could never be perfect nor did I want to be perfect! I didn't even want to be nearly perfect!

My goodness, you say, what will mainstream medicine come to if there are no more "super-nurses" and "doctor-gods"?

Well, my friend, read on.

In the two years that followed, through my experiences with Rosen Work, counseling, the twelve-step program of Adult Children of Alcoholics, Bioenergetic Breathing technique, Taoism, Yoga, and other experiential, holistic, and spiritual paths, I began to heal myself and learn to be present for the healing of others. My life began to change when I realized that I had choices and did not have to be a victim of circumstances. I recognized that growing up in a dysfunctional home as the eldest child, my role had been that of caretaker, so I naturally gravitated toward a profession where I could hope to "save" people. Encountering my own rage, pain, fear, and mortality, I was able to gradually accept what I had thought was my "dark" side. In my growing self-acceptance blossomed new personal power and the letting go of wanting to control others. I put less and less blame on others and the "system" and took more responsibility for my life. My own hands-on work evolved into what I simply called Touch and I opened a private practice, lectured, and taught others to Touch.

Chapter 8

What is Touch?

Touch is very powerful and really nothing new, having been used for thousands of years in different forms of the healing arts. Some patients begin Touch to relieve physical pain, some because of stress or emotional pain and others because they want to learn to care for and know themselves. Whatever the motivation, all that's needed is a willingness to be with oneself and to look within.

Medical science readily agrees that psychological, emotional and physical stressors cause a great number of illnesses and ailments. Through my own and my patients' experiences with Touch, I have learned that our bodies are one of our greatest resources for optimum health and personal growth. They are the living history books of our lives, containing forgotten experiences and unconscious feelings and attitudes. Many of these unconscious beliefs and feelings from our past experiences direct our responses and actions in our present lives. Conditioned response is the scientific term for this and it was first demonstrated in the famous Pavlov experiment: Immediately before the dogs were fed, a bell was rung. After continuing this routine for some time, the dogs were <u>not</u> fed after the bell was rung. They still, however, salivated and had all of the physical responses that they would have had before eating. So the ringing of the bell, caused a conditioned response in the dogs, even though there was actually no food.

We feel in our bodies but our minds are the powerful censors of our feelings. Censoring or blocking feelings, often along with the conscious memories, is the mechanism that allows us to survive traumatic or painful situations. What happens to all of the unfelt feelings? They are put away in the body where they become an unconscious physical holding or tension in the tissues, muscles and organs.

An example of this unconscious learned holding or conditioned response is toilet training. We are taught at a very young age through reward or punishment, to hold our urinary and anal sphincter muscles. Now we are experiencing a learned holding that was unconscious until I just brought your attention to it. Here's another example: a little boy starts to cry because he is hurt. His father says, "Stop crying! Big boys don't cry!" The little boy wants his father's love and approval so he holds back his sobs by tightening his throat and neck muscles and swallowing hard. After years of keeping sadness or pain inside, it becomes an unconscious conditioned response and remains held in the throat, neck and upper chest. This same response occurs in different related areas of the body for other feelings that are "unacceptable." Something to keep in mind, though, is that often "unacceptable" can also be exuberance, laughter, joy and other "positive" feelings as well. Eventually, as with Pavlov's dogs, there is no more conscious connection, no more "food" to cause the physical response, only the stimulus of the "bell" to cause a conditioned response. The reason or cause between the actual feeling and its physical response is non-existent. This is why as adults we may often feel like we are wearing a mask and going through the motions of living.

Most of the time, we are unaware of the tension we are holding in our bodies until it becomes painful. Most of us say, "Yes, but I injured that area, that's why it hurts." Areas in our body that are holding these "conditioned memories" are tense and inflexible so those are the areas that are most likely to be injured.

Marion Rosen, once told a story about a woman who had sustained a severe leg injury in an accident. Two years after the accident, the injury long since healed, her doctors were baffled by the limp with which the woman still walked. After much testing and head scratching, they referred her to Marion, who was a Physical Therapist. Marion asked the woman to walk for her which she did and, after several minutes of observing her, Marion asked, "Does it hurt you to walk?" to which the woman answered that it did not.

Why are you limping?" Marion asked.

"Am I limping? I didn't know that!" and she walked again, without the limp, thanked Marion and left the office. No one had ever asked this woman the obvious, they just assumed that because she was limping that she was in pain! For the woman it had just become a conditioned response from that time when she was in pain.

As in the above story, we sometimes have areas of tension and guarding in our bodies that remain unnecessarily long after the pain of the original trauma has subsided. Often all a person needs is to become aware of the unconscious conditioned response that is being held in the body. When an area of stress or pain in the body is touched during a session, the patient is able to focus on that area. Through touch as well as words, the experiencing of the actual feeling is emphasized. The patient is encouraged to stay with the present feeling, to allow it to be for the moment, with a possibility, but not necessity, of consciously recognizing the feeling and perhaps, a related incident.

As a nurse practicing Touch, I first do a nursing assessment which is an evaluation of my patients physical condition by noting his color, objective and subjective comfort and symptoms as well as checking vital signs. After completing my "nurse stuff" and asking permission to touch the area of stress or pain, I address what I see, feel and sense in my patient's body. For example, after I have been doing Touch for some time, I may notice that my patient has a pounding heart, short, shallow breaths and perspiration, so I will bring his attention to what's occurring in his body. I may then suggest that these physical responses could be connected to fear. If this suggestion is true for the patient, his body will respond in any number of ways through perhaps a sob, sigh, tremor, softening or tensing, when I say the word. If it has no meaning for that person, there will be no physical response. I will again report back to the patient with something like, "Yes, fear seems like it has meaning for you. Your body just responded to the word fear. What are you noticing?"

One of the questions I'm asked most often is "So how will feeling all of those painful, uncomfortable feelings help me?"

As a patient reexperiences on a conscious level, the incidents and related feelings that were unsafe to experience at the time of the occurrence, there is an actual physical softening of the once tense or painful areas in the body. As more breath and blood enters these areas, the patient will often experience more space, a lightness or a feeling of peace. Along with the physical release, there is often a time of self-acceptance with these moments that eventually extends and carries over into the patient's life. Carl Rogers wrote, "When I accept myself, then I change." When we can begin to allow ourselves to be vulnerable with another human being, to be seen, to drop the masks and accept who we really are, changes just happen naturally and without any effort at all!

Chapter 9

Why Touch Works

Mosby's Medical dictionary defines Touch Deprivation as "a lack of tactile stimulation, especially in early infancy, which if continued for a sufficient length of time may lead to serious developmental and emotional disturbances, such as stunted growth, personality disorders and social regression. In severe cases, a child who is deprived of adequate physical handling and emotional stimulation may not survive infancy."

Touch is recognized and accepted by medical science as necessary for normal growth and development. People of all ages need to be touched. Nurturing touch increases warmth and movement in the body, connects us to ourselves and each other and opens us to communication on all levels. Touch creates a caring environment, decreases stress, and promotes feelings of self-acceptance, a sense of well-being, and positive mental attitude, which studies have found result in better functioning of our immune systems.

In our culture, what we get most often in our adult lives is sexual touch, or no touch at all. Sex, in its reciprocity, is no substitute for true acceptance through nurturing touch. Because so many adults are touch deprived, it's no wonder there is so much media focus on sex. Parents who were not held and physically nurtured as children are unable to nurture their own children. Sexual addictions, adultery, incest, pornography, impotence, prostitution, mental illness and other addictions and dysfunctions are a direct result of nurturing-touch deprivation. Too often nurturing touch has been replaced with inappropriate sexual and abusive touch. Many physical, emotional and psychological illnesses are the result of touch deprivation or inappropriate/abusive touch.

Failure to thrive could easily apply to older adults and the elderly in the forms of loss of appetite and malnutrition, insomnia, memory loss and senility, agitation and depression. Working in convalescent homes over the years, I would all too frequently see a normal, mentally clear elderly person admitted to the institution and within two weeks, that person would be mentally confused, incontinent and wearing diapers and so agitated that often tranquilizers and physical restraints would be needed for safety.

One Christmas day, my friend, Jonathan and I were visiting his grandmother in the nursing home where she has been a resident for seven years. We found her in the day room in a purple and pink flower print dress. She recognized her grandson and when he introduced me, I extended my hand which she seized and didn't release. She held it tight, even as Jonathan wheeled her to her room, where it was quieter, so the three of us could visit. Jonathan had brought her flowers, so I offered to put them in a vase with water before I sat down to talk with them. Jonathan had told me before we arrived, that Gram had been confused for most of the last six years. She repeatedly mumbled, "Oh, dear" and occasionally would let out an unsettling wailing sound. Gram was fidgety and rocked back and forth making a half circle with her wheelchair. After we had looked at all of the family photographs on her wall and dresser, Jonathan was at a loss as to what to say. When she spoke, there were many moments of confusion and she was distracted and vague, but for the most part she was silent. Jonathan seemed uncomfortable and cleared his throat several times.

When I noticed that her hands were quite chapped, I asked her if I could put some lotion on them. She agreed. After warming the moisturizer in my hand, I held the bottle toward Jonathan. We each took a hand and gently massaged.

After a few minutes, Gram smiled and sighed, "I feel, I feel...like a queen." And indeed, she looked regal.

Ten minutes later, I noticed that her body was relaxing and that her rocking back and forth had stopped. She laughed easily, spoke with more conviction and was very present and focused. Her "Oh dears" and wails had ceased. In about another five minutes, she began to glance out into the hallway with some concern.

"What will people think?" she asked.

"Do you mean, if they see you getting your hands massaged?" I asked.

"Yes."

"Do you want us to stop?"

"Yes, I think it's best that you do," she replied.

When we released her hands, she lifted them up and studied them with great amazement and interest, turning them over, sideways and back, inspecting every part.

"What's the matter, Gram?" Jonathan asked.

"Ooooo," she marveled softly, "they feel so good, especially the right one." As she continued to stare at them for some time, I grinned over at Jonathan, sitting on her left.

This was only fifteen minutes of touch on someone whose only day to day experience of touch had been for hygienic maintenance. The response was simple, subtle and powerful.

CHAPTER 10

TOUCH EQUALS SEX, RIGHT?

There are many people who see touch and sex as one and the same. Touch is sensual so touch most certainly can be sexual. I have had some sexual feelings of my own when I have been receiving massage or other types of hands-on work as well as when doing Touch. Many times patients will comment that they are feeling sexual when they are receiving a Touch session.

Sexual feelings are normal and natural and so are appropriate expressions of those feelings. When I have had them as a receiver of hands-on work, I have acknowledged them, explored them and moved on. Back when I was "nearly perfect" I was obsessively focused on sexuality and my relationships with men, due to my unconscious, unresolved personal issues. Touch has helped me to be with, then move through the pain. I am now able to focus on my relationship with myself and have begun to create the life that I have always wanted.

Very often, both men and women patients I have worked on, have had sexual feelings come up during a session, feelings about incest or abuse and Touch has helped them greatly. Because sex and physical abuse involves body contact, and the body stores memories, Touch will very often uncover unconscious feelings and memories around these issues. Touch can and does stir sexual memories and is evocative but it is not provocative.

Obviously, incest, sexual abuse and physical abuse among others are all inappropriate touch. The only appropriate sexual contact is that between consenting adults of sound mind.

As with any professional, be it nurses, doctors, dentists, psychiatrists or therapists, when clients come for a Touch session, they are coming for help, for relief of some pain or problem. It's not the Touch "technique" but rather two people (or more) coming together in love that heals. As the practitioner of Touch, I am the professional and it's up to me to maintain professional standards. The patient comes to me and for the time he or she is on the table, they are vulnerable and open and it's up to me to honor that vulnerability, not to violate it.

Conversely, I expect the same from my patients. On a few occasions with male patients, I have had to remind them of this. Once, while doing Touch on a man in my office, he remarked that he was having sexual feelings towards me. I acknowledged his feelings and clearly stated that his feelings were okay but any action on them were not. He was lying on his stomach at that time, my hands were on his back, as I stood next to the table. A few minutes later, he reached out and wrapped his right arm around my leg, holding my calf with his hand.

"You'll have to take your hand off of my leg or this session is over," I said.

He apologized and immediately removed his hand.

"I know you said you were having sexual feelings toward me, before," I said, "but maybe you could tell me how it is for you to be lying on the table here with me touching you and you not able to touch me."

He talked about how difficult it was for him to be lying on the table because he was feeling so passive. As an executive of a large corporation, he was used to being in charge at work, and in all of his relationships. I then asked him how he felt about me setting some limits on our relationship and he said he was angry. So I asked him to be with the anger and the session was quite wonderful and revealing and it resulted in relaxation and low back pain relief.

Feelings of vulnerability and tenderness

Greg a tall, attractive man with a thick head of salt and pepper gray hair was a psychotherapist in his mid fifties. His main complaint was that of low back pain and general tension and he found Touch relieved them.

During his sessions, there seemed to come a point where he would recognize some feelings of pain and vulnerability, and experience some brief moments of tenderness and then immediately report that he had an erection. This seemed to be something that reoccurred over the year that Greg had Touch sessions. On those occasions, I would suggest to him that his tender feelings were immediately replaced by sexual ones, bringing his focus away from his heart and into his genitals. Often angered by this observation and directing it towards me, I would always try to help him bring the focus back onto himself. Generally he would, as many do when faced with uncomfortable feelings, bring his attention to what someone was doing to him, how someone was making him feel, rather than recognizing that those feelings belonged to him.

All of us are unique and different. If it fits, we know it, if not, it will roll off of our backs like water off of a duck. From my experience, though there have been exceptions, it seems that many gender-related similarities are true. In our society, it is generally less acceptable for a man to cry, be sensitive and express tender feelings, just as it is less acceptable for a woman to be assertive or angry. Generally, sexuality for a man is more active than passive.

People like Greg, having experienced feelings of vulnerability or tenderness, will often immediately and unconsciously translate them into feelings of sexuality. This takes them from a perceived "scary" place, a place of vulnerability which is actually a place that allows us to truly love and be loved (not always sexual) to a place of sexual "action" where they feel more in "control." Of course any kind of real love also has to come from this place of openness and vulnerability, but again, it's back to the black and white kind of thinking: sex equals touch, so touch equals sex and along with that is love equal sex and sex equals love.

So when Greg felt those feelings of tenderness, vulnerability and love, it was interpreted as sex, because in our culture sex equals love, doesn't it? Well that's what so many of our movies, songs, books and television shows tell us.

What Greg may have been experiencing was self love. I experienced my first feelings of true self love and simply love of life and love of love, while having hands-on work. This has since flowed over into almost everything that I do, filling my life completely and fully. When I first experienced this wonderful, scary feeling of well-being and universal love, it felt sexual to me, too. It's a wonderful, warm, glowing feeling and it's there if we allow ourselves to be open to it. It's what we all are searching for, and it's right here with us now, if we open our hearts. The only kind of "love" that I had heard about, read about, heard sung about and experienced was the romantic "love," sexual "love" and that was all that there was.

When I was in my late twenties, I had a relationship with a man with whom I discovered that wonderful, sexual side of myself that I didn't know existed. It was fun, playful, creative and exciting and that's what the relationship was like, too. Then, after three years, he was killed in an accident. I mourned the loss of him for years, and I mourned the loss of my sexuality and the love that I believed had been buried with him.

Six years later, at a Yoga retreat, I had an experience that changed me: There were about one hundred of us in the chapel and we were doing a Yoga "free flow," which is, after holding a particular posture for as long as possible, you release the posture, keeping your eyes closed and allow your body to move where it wants and needs to move. Releasing the posture, I moved into the free flow, and my body moved slowly on the floor, turning, stretching, twisting in luscious sensation. My eyes were closed and I heard the soft music. I could feel the sun warming my face as I stretched and turned over onto my back and suddenly I felt overwhelmed with emotion because I was aware of how beautiful, sensual and sexual I felt as I lay there luxuriating and reveling in the sensations and movements in my own body. Only then did it occur to me that I was a sensual and sexual being in and of myself and I didn't need anyone to make me feel that way because I always was and always would be. Up until that moment in time, I believed that unless there was an object of love and sexuality, I could not be sexual, sensual, beautiful and loved. So suddenly, I was not only lovable, sensual, sexual and beautiful, love was all around me and inside of me... I *was* Love!

Sexual, romantic love is wonderful but, though the media may not want us to believe it, consider that it is only a small percentage of the Love available to us all.

For years I thought that romantic, love relationships were the only kind that existed and spent most of my time and energy beginning them, staying in them, or leaving them. Today, I highly recommend having a love relationship with yourself, first. Being with all of who you are. At first, I found it to be often painful and difficult. Once I was able to observe myself without judgment, I began to like myself little by little and actually started to get a kick out of those parts of myself that I tried to hide, especially my anger. I started to see my anger as a friend, a little warning light that helped me become aware of when I needed to set limits (something I was never taught to do as a child). My anger is one of those parts of myself that helped me survive to that point. I need and still need my anger and I have learned to recognize, accept and express it appropriately most of the time.

Feelings are a wonderful part of being human, but they are just feelings and not who we really are. We have feelings but we are not our feelings. Being with our feelings can, at first, be painful and scary because it is dark and unknown. Though I didn't know it for years, I know now, that it's okay to be afraid.

When I was a child I was afraid of the dark and was terrified of going into our cellar alone. Often, though, I did descend those creaking, wooden stairs because I believed that I was not supposed to be afraid and was ashamed to show my fear. Once the light had been turned on in the cellar, I recognized the harmless objects that had been foreboding shadows in the darkness, but I usually grabbed what I had come for and ran quickly back up the stairs. I was sure that something terrible would spring at me from behind the furnace or some other dark place. None of us have to go into our "cellars" alone and because we still believe we do, often spend years standing at the top of the stairs. So on your journey of self-discovery and healing, whether it be Touch or any other path, allow someone to touch you, to take your hand with love; your pain will be lessened and your joys will be multiplied.

CHAPTER 11

KNOWING THAT WE DON'T KNOW

When I first started practicing Touch, I would often find myself working deeper and harder on a client, feeling irritated that nothing seemed to be happening. I wasn't doing it "right," I'd think. This person is paying me so I have to DO something, to fix her, I have to earn my money. When I'd catch myself doing this, I'd say to my client:

"Now, I'm going to take my hands off of you for a little while, and you tell me what you notice, once they're off." And we'd continue the session like that for awhile, and I'd say to myself, "See, this person is getting what they need and having a good session without you doing anything at all." And then, I'd put my hands back on, and I'd notice that I wasn't trying to fix them anymore.

It was very difficult at first, to forget what I thought I knew and to be in the unknown. Because this is what I suggest that my clients and patients do, I have to do it, too. So my intention is really to have no intention. It's more just wanting to be with a person - just that, to BE. To be a gentle presence, to not judge and to affirm who they are and what they are feeling in the moment. It is to be in the present, without ego, a witness to another person's unfolding. Just to be with what is, in and of itself, is profound and healing.

If I am in that place, in the moment, accepting and without judgment, my Touch, or whatever I may be offering that person, will reflect that.

Though in a place of "not knowing" I do know one thing: that there is a higher intelligence that is present and guides us all on our own individual journeys. This knowledge is not an intellectual "knowing" but rather an inner knowing. Some call this higher intelligence God, others call it nature, intuition, life force, Great Spirit, and many other names. I call it Love. Though many of the choices my patients make may not be those that I would make, I can lovingly offer my ideas and suggestions, knowing that the choice is theirs. The illness or injury is not the enemy but rather that person's present experience. As a health care professional, I see my job to be that of "advisor" chosen to participate in "peace talks" which are a meeting of minds and spirits. Picture the patient seated at a conference table with his doctor and other related specialists of his choice. The patient, as commander-in-chief, is at the head of the table, with his "advisors" around him. All heads are turned in the patient's direction, all ears are listening intently, honoring his opinions and feelings about his impending treatment.

The patient is the one in charge, he makes the final decisions regarding his body and his life. The "advisors," though they may not agree with his decisions, will support him by being there for him and honoring his decision. Conversely, I think it is important for the patient to respect the "advisors" he chooses and carefully consider all of the options presented to him.

I am as honest as possible at all times, and if I am concerned about them in any way, I tell them so in a respectful way, such as "I'm really concerned about you being here all alone tonight because you're feeling dizzy. I'm worried that you might fall and no one will be here to help you." Or, I may strongly suggest that a patient see her doctor, follow a prescribed treatment or diet, or go to the hospital.

Medical science has come a long way and certainly surgery, procedures, medications and other therapy are indispensable but, in the scheme of things, there is really very little we can actually DO for another person. Healing begins when a person starts to take responsibility for themselves and make choices about their bodies, minds and spirits. I used to believe my job was to make the patient realize what was best for them because then, there was only one way. What a relief to finally learn that I can only offer suggestions, but the responsibility of choice belongs to them. My responsibility is to do the best job I can as a nurse and then be there for my patient as another human being on the journey of life. Once the surgery is done, the medication is taken, the care plan is in place, there is much time that is needed for healing. Then, I see myself as a witness, someone to encourage, affirm and applaud each step my patients take as they follow their own path of healing.

In his book, The Undiscovered Self, Carl Jung wrote, "In view of the fact that in principle, the positive advantages of knowledge work specifically to the disadvantage of understanding, the judgment resulting therefrom is likely to be something of a paradox. Judged scientifically, the individual is nothing but a unit which repeats itself ad infinitum and could just as well be designated with a letter of the alphabet. For understanding, on the other hand, it is just the unique individual human being who, when stripped of all those conformities and regularities so dear to the heart of the scientist, is the supreme and only real object of investigation. The doctor, above all, should be aware of this contradiction. On the one hand, he is equipped with the statistical truths of his scientific training, and on the other, he is faced with the task of treating a sick person who, especially in the case of psychic suffering, requires individual understanding. The more schematic the treatment is, the more the resistances it – quite rightly – calls up in the patient and the more the cure is jeopardized."

With few exceptions, medical science, insurance companies and HMOs see the patient as a diagnosis or a code with a predictable course of treatment and a predictable outcome. The intention, therefore, is to fix this patient as a mechanic would fix a car. The belief is that there is something wrong with this patient and the cure comes from the medication or procedure, that one patient is the same as the next just as each car manufactured is the essentially the same. With human beings, this is far from the truth.

When I know that I don't know, I have set the stage for both myself and my patients to be alert and open to new changes in the body and in our individual experiences. If I am trying to solve the mystery, but I believe that I already know not only what the mystery is, but also what caused it, would I even notice if there were any changes? Would I be alert to new clues? Would I be able to help bring that person's attention to it? Of course not. It would merely be like conducting a "study" to prove some foregone conclusion.

Chapter 12

To Be or Not to Be

The word *be* is defined as "to exist in actuality; have reality or life." Isn't this the goal of most therapy? Simple, but we often find the most difficulty in the simplest things. With every Touch session there is learning and healing for both patient and practitioner. The practitioner who analyzes and diagnoses, rather than being present is ineffective in facilitating healing. The patient who needs to know, "What's wrong with me and how are you going to fix it?" is denying his being and relinquishing his personal power.

Being is often as quiet as a summer wind or can vibrate like thunder. There is no right or wrong way to be. Being can be very elusive and subtle at first and for most, very uncomfortable. Being can be excruciatingly painful physically, emotionally and spiritually before it becomes joyful, playful and spontaneous. In allowing ourselves to be, we are in the present and in the unknown, and we are then empowered and can heal whatever needs to be healed in us.

The only difference between the practitioner of Touch and the patient is that the patient is being touched and experiences being, and if she wants, talks about that experience. The practitioner has her hands on that person, is fully present in the moment and listens with her heart. Ideally, both are present and fully in touch with their physical selves, because that is where we feel – in our bodies. When we feel angry or excited, our hearts beat faster, our breathing increases, muscles tense, jaws often tighten and faces may flush. With sadness, throats tighten, we swallow hard, breathing becomes labored and sporadic, chins may quiver, diaphragms tremor and sob and tears fill our eyes. Fear often causes the skin to be cold and clammy, the breath to be held, the heart to pound causing the entire body to vibrate and face to pale. These are all physical manifestations of feelings. When we as children, and later as socialized adults, learn to hold back these feelings, they remain locked in our bodies as unconscious memories. Held in the constantly tight musculature and tissues, this adversely affects our breathing and the circulation of body fluids. This impaired function can eventually cause pain and illness but in the meantime, these are all tipoffs for the practitioner of Touch: areas where the skin is cool, muscles are tight and breathing is decreased or absent are areas where feelings are being held. Conversely, areas that may be warmer than the rest of the body, could also be "hot spots" of held feelings. These are the areas that the practitioner will focus on.

The wise adage, "If it's not broken, don't fix it" applies with Touch. Though a patient may feel "broken" when they come for therapy, the truth is, they have lost touch with their true selves. We already have all that we need for healing if we are willing to be in our bodies, in the moment and to acknowledge that our feelings exist. We don't have to like them, but they need to be recognized. It is not about analyzing. If the physical feeling is recognized but no conscious connection is made, it is alright! We stay in the being, not in the knowing intellectually. Both patient and practitioner need to be with what IS. Very often the unconscious memory is pre-verbal, in that the connected incident occurred when the patient was an infant or toddler, before they could speak, so there are no words to associate with the feeling. So the practitioner just encourages the patient to just be with whatever is happening. This requires patience, trust and love. Perhaps the connected feeling is too painful for the patient to reexperience at that time. We need to trust that when the patient is ready, the memory will present itself.

The definition of the word feel is "To perceive, give or produce through the sense of touch." Touch helps the patient focus on the physical manifestations that she may be experiencing and very often a conscious connection is then made to the associated unconscious feelings that have been so tightly and often painfully held in her body. In that moment of acceptance, comes the space and possibility for conscious choice and transformation.

What a thing man is! Among all wonders,
the wonder of the world is man himself.

—Sophocles

PART FOUR

guerrilla nursing

CHAPTER 13

BACK IN THE MAINSTREAM

I loved being a part of the holistic health community but two years later, I was drawn back into mainstream medicine. Modern medical science has much to offer in the way of diagnosing, treatment, surgery, and medications with knowledge and skill that is truly amazing, especially in cases of acute illness and trauma. There are many caring and well-intentioned healthcare professionals: I was one of them. It was never that I had lost faith in the basis of modern medical science, it was just that it was lacking something very important: the human Touch. Now I wanted to incorporate a more holistic and spiritual approach into the medical model of healthcare, sure that my personal healing experiences and those of my clients were proof positive. Mainstream medical treatment when needed, along with Touch (as a complementary therapy) on a regular basis for health maintenance, is a great combination. Returning to nursing would give me the opportunity to affirm what I already knew to be true: I finally had something to offer patients that would make a difference—my humanity and my touch.

It seemed that there was an exclusivity, if not distrust and outright discrediting of one another, between the disciplines of holistic, mainstream and spiritual healing. As the daughter of a Christian Scientist, I was raised in a world where mainstream medicine and religion were at war and it seemed to me that the war escalated when I became a nurse and then later when I started to explore holistic healing methods. Modern medicine, religion, psychology, and "alternative methods" all appeared to be proclaiming that their way was the only way. The war was over the means and the end – the patient's health of body, mind, and spirit – was forgotten.

The letters, proposals, and information on Touch I sent to doctors, administrators, and institutions met with little interest. Meetings with directors of nurses and medical boards came down to questions of reimbursement. Demonstrations of Touch for my colleagues were politely but coolly received. A large percentage of the patients they were seeing openly expressed their dissatisfaction with, and often outright hostility toward, mainstream medical care. These patients wanted more from healthcare but were afraid to try alternative methods.

I think of my mother's struggle to define herself and her health in relation to mainstream medicine and Christian Science, both, in essence, demanding that she make a choice between one or the other. What we all need right now is a healthy blend of mainstream medicine, complementary methods and spirituality. Though often referred to as "alternative" methods, I prefer to call them "complementary" instead. I strongly feel that there is no ONE way to health and healing and I want to stay open to any new ideas and therapies. Some of the complementary therapies could include, but not be limited to education in nutrition, herbal and vitamin therapies, stress management, exercise and lifestyle change as well as Touch, massage and psychotherapy (both traditional and non), acupuncture, Yoga, meditation and any other therapy that may sound appealing and/or feel right. We all need to try new things and decide for ourselves if they are right for us.

It comes down to something quite simple: each of us taking responsibility for our own health: health of our bodies, minds and spirits. Simple but not easy.

A patient of mine, Josephine, lived alone in a senior housing development since the death of her husband twelve years before. In her late sixties, she wore her blonde hair teased up in a bun and a pink and purple floral house dress with matching pink lipstick. She had been visited every two weeks by a home care nurse for blood pressure checks and pre-pouring of her medications.

"Your blood pressure is 150/88," I told her on one morning visit, "about what you normally run and your heart and lungs sound fine today."

She smiled and nodded. I asked her if she had any complaints, problems, questions or anything else that she'd like to talk about.

"Well, I do have a little heartburn today," she replied.

"What did you have for breakfast?" I asked her.

"Coffee, orange juice, and a muffin."

"Do you usually eat that?"

"Well, I did have an extra cup of coffee not long ago."

"Maybe that didn't agree with you. Coffee is quite acid and so is orange juice. You might try not drinking the coffee or juice tomorrow, or maybe skip the extra cup. Stress can also increase the secretion of excess digestive acids. Is there something stressful going on in your life right now?"

Josephine sighed and waved her hand impatiently, clearly signaling that she wanted nothing more to do with the conversation. Then she said, "Isn't there just a pill you can give me?"

Wouldn't it be great if it were as easy as taking a pill? Well, I have learned that Dr. Seynour's pink "bubble gum" medicine doesn't always work. Health and well-being depend on many things and first and foremost is personal power and responsibility to ourselves. It's a commitment to health of the body, mind and spirit that requires living consciously and becoming aware of the needs of all three.

"Kaboshed by the powers that be..."

My first job back in mainstream medicine was as a part-time nursing supervisor in a long-term care facility. In many ways it was a difficult position because the nurses and nurses aides that I supervised were all members of the local Teamsters Union. Union staff and management were always at odds and though the staff's pay was the highest in the area, morale was always low. I was non-union and of course all of my superiors were "management." I was in Never Never Land, between a rock and hard place. But this was also the place where I began to do

Touch on patients in a mainstream medical setting.

First, I had tried to introduce the idea to the director of nursing and administrator of the facility and both humored me by listening but, as they saw it, had their own problems. I had suggested Touch be used for patients and staff as well, and even offered to do some at no charge on a trial basis. Touch, I assured them, would greatly help the patients and would also raise morale among the staff. To make a very long story short, they weren't interested. So I simply began offering it to patients and was thrilled with the results!

I wrote letters to other long-term care facilities, hospitals and doctors, again offering my time free of charge on a trial basis and again, I had no takers. Some of the responses, if they did respond, were concerns about liability and reimbursement.

Working as a home care nurse, where I could visit with patients one on one in their homes, I decided, seemed like the ideal way to incorporate Touch into the mainstream medical system. I found a per diem job that would give me the flexibility to continue with my private practice in Touch, as well as my research, writing, and lectures. After working with a Connecticut home-care agency for six months, I offered to do an in-service on Touch for the nursing staff and all who had patient contact and was asked to put it in a letter of proposal by the administrator. Once submitted, I had no response for several months. When I approached her and questioned her about it, she apologized saying that she wasn't ignoring me, it was just that well, it was summer and people were on vacations and she just hadn't had time. She would definitely be back to me in the fall. Well September came and went with no word. One day, Paula, the community health nurse, acting on her own, asked me if I would give a lecture on Touch at an area Senior Center the following month, which I happily agreed to do. All was arranged and when the director of the agency was informed, she asked that their public relations person do some publicity about it for the newspapers. A writer was sent to interview me and we spent two hours together. He was very enthusiastic and wrote a beautiful story about the work, quoting a client of mine: "Linda placed her hands gently on my back..." and "she lovingly guided me through painful childhood memories."

A few days later, Paula came to me and told me that she was completely disgusted. The story "had been kaboshed by the powers that be" and would not be published because someone at the top had decided that Touch was "provocative and sexual." Though neither the director nor the public relations person had had any experience with, nor knowledge of Touch, they had declared that they would not promote it. To their dismay, however, it was too late to cancel my upcoming speaking engagement. The presentation was well attended and I was enthusiastically received at the Senior Center.

A few days later, a thank-you note arrived from their executive director: "There was obviously a lot of interest in your program and several people stopped to tell me how much they appreciated hearing you. Most of us know that we should slow down and be more 'in tune' with ourselves, but it is helpful to be reminded that this is also a good thing for our health and well-being. I have always been impressed with the caliber of nurses at your agency and their dedication to health education in our community. Thank you for being a part of this tradition..."

The minutes from the staff meeting at the home care agency the following week read: "Nurses at our agency may only function within the scope of nursing practice. Things such as touch therapy and attitudinal adjustments are not within this scope. Stress management may only be provided as part of a nursing visit and not as the sole reason for a prolonged visit. There is no reimbursement mechanism for such visits. Our approach must stay within the medical model. We may only provide professional care to our patients. We may not do things with patients on 'off duty' time such as take shopping, dinner etc...." In that moment, I decided that I was not waiting for permission anymore. It occurred to me that change in healthcare would have to be like any lasting change – from the inside out.

By this time, I was tired of writing letters and proposals anyway. I was sick to death of "proper channels" and attempting to get the blessing of the "powers that be" (whoever they are). So when I read the staff meeting minutes (I had had the good fortune of not being at that meeting), I made a decision: I would do it anyway! Even if the administrators were not interested, my patients were and I was in the perfect position. As a home care nurse, my job was to visit people in their homes, do physical assessments, dressing changes, blood drawing, medication review, teaching and all those other required nursing tasks for which I was trained and did well. But, I was one on one with my patients and there was always time to incorporate some Touch into my visit if they wanted it. I began charting vital signs before and after Touch and found (though it didn't surprise me in the least) that it lowered high blood pressure, eased shortness of breath and slowed heart rates. My colleagues began referring patients to me who had migraines, depression, anxiety, or those with pain. To this day, none of the patients that I have offered Touch to have refused. In fact, they almost always would ask me to do it again, each time I visited. (And those that didn't ask, would say when I offered, "Oh, I didn't want to ask because I didn't want to take up more of your time.") There is always time for Touch. So after I do all of my "nurse stuff" that is within the "medical model," I put on my "camos" and take to the trees for a little "Guerrilla Nursing" (though didn't I hear somewhere that nursing is a "hands-on" profession?).

Chapter 14

Porcupines Need Love, Too

Her stone house reminded me of the way Miss Havisham's house may have looked in the novel "Great Expectations." I found Catherine sitting amongst the clutter in the darkest corner of her huge dining room eating a salad, muttering complaints between each mouthful about the help being incompetent, stupid and not knowing how to make a decent salad. Her posture, from the base of her neck to the top of her head, was held in an almost a horizontal position so that I had to sit on a chair and bend forward to meet her eyes when she would occasionally lift them from under wisps of white hair.

"You're too old to be wearing your hair that long," were the first words out of her mouth.

"I like it this way," I replied, trying not to show my irritation.

"These girls I have are completely useless, as you all are," she grumbled as her home health aide standing behind her, rolled her eyes, sighed and left the room. She continued on a long monologue about the ineptness of nurses, aides and doctors, specifically and in general with strategically placed personal attacks, though we had never met before. As I listened, I felt anger building inside of me and thought that I'd like to check her over quickly and make this visit as short as possible. It crossed my mind that this woman who lived alone and needed people, was doing everything possible to drive them away. I had been warned by my colleagues that this was a "difficult" patient that nobody wanted to visit and her reputation was such that it was almost impossible to get a nurse's aide to care for her. We all need love but it seems that those who need it most are the most difficult to "touch." Though I wanted to touch her neck, another part of me wanted to head out of the door. What I wanted more was to touch her. I would be of no help to her if I just kept my mouth shut, so I decided to let my curiosity lead the way:

"Have you always been this angry?" I asked.

Momentarily taken aback, she hesitated, then said, "Well, no, no, of course not. It's just that I'm in pain all of the time, that's why I'm cross."

"It must be terrible to be in constant pain."

"Well, yes, yes it is," she replied, lifting her blue eyes to mine. "I'm angry that no one has helped me. In fact they've made it worse. I've been to all of the best doctors and clinics and spent a fortune on medical expenses and look at me! They say to me, 'Well, you're eighty-one, what do you expect?' I want to feel good!"

"Of course." I took a breath. Well, here goes: "Would it be alright if I touched your neck very gently? I do a little hands-on work."

To my delight, she agreed. There was a vertical surgical scar the entire length of her neck which was flat as a board from its base to her head, with absolutely no cervical curve making her unable to hold her head upright. The painfully tight muscles in her neck and shoulders were like steel under my hands.

After perhaps three or four minutes of silence, Catherine sighed, then said softly, "You have given me more attention than any of the doctors that I have been to."

We were quiet a little longer, then I felt some very subtle movement in her neck muscles. She sighed again and told me that she was raised by deaf parents whom she cared for in many ways along with a younger brother. After her parents' deaths, she and her brother lived together in the big house until eight years ago when he died of a heart attack. Many of the stories she told were filled with sadness and pain.

"It sounds like there's been a lot of pain in your life," I commented.

Her neck muscles softened very slightly under my hands, returned to steel momentarily, then began to pulsate here and there with very subtle movement. Then, she said, "I don't know why, but somehow just knowing that someone understands how much pain I'm in makes me feel better. The pain has actually lessened."

She told me that a doctor at a world famous clinic had removed five disks in her cervical (neck area) spine and that a specialist, whom she had seen since then, felt that the surgery had only worsened her condition. Catherine had computerized copies of her entire extensive medical history which she showed me as I continued to keep my hands on her neck and shoulders, listening and acknowledging her feelings.

"You know that comment that I made about your hair being too long for someone your age?" she said.

"Yes?"

"Well, I take it back."

I laughed and suddenly felt so much love for Catherine that I spontaneously hugged her, then kissed her cheek. It was as if a porcupine had pulled in her quills and I could feel the softness of fur instead.

The next time I visited Catherine, I was so happy to see her, I moved right towards her and gave her a hug. She stiffened and I realized that in my enthusiasm, I had not asked her for permission, but it was too late.

"Do you always hug everyone you see?" she grumbled angrily.

"Oh, I'm really sorry that I didn't ask you first and I apologize," I said, sitting down on the little stool near her feet so I could see her eyes. "I was just really happy to see you again."

"Well, I guess it's okay," she said with a sigh. "I've just been upset with Lena. She thinks she can bake and she can't! And now she's made brownies!"

"They smell good."

"Well, maybe they are. Do you want to try one?"

"Sure. Do you want one, too?"

"Well, maybe just to try it."

I went to the kitchen and cut some brownies from the pan. They were still warm and full of plump walnuts. After putting them on plates and getting some napkins and forks, I returned to the dining room.

"How about some tea with your brownie?" Catherine asked.

"Good idea," I replied and made us some tea.

After our tea and brownie party, I gave Catherine her calcium injection, checked vital signs and did a physical assessment and reviewed her medications. Then I asked her if she wanted me to do some Touch on her again.

"Yes, I'd like that, but only if you have the time. It does help."

I gently placed my hands on her neck of steel and we were, for the most part, silent. Occasionally Catherine would ask me what I was feeling under my hands and often I would ask her what she noticed when I felt a change in her neck: sometimes there would be a trembling feeling, then maybe some pulsating and a subtle softening before it would turn to steel again. I kept my hands in gentle contact for maybe fifteen minutes before letting her know that I would be stopping soon and then slowly took my hands off of her neck.
"It really does help," she repeated.

"I'm glad. Thank you."

"No, thank you!" she smiled up at me, her blue eyes softer, now.

As I gathered my things to go, Catherine got up and using her walker, shuffled into the kitchen. "Now, I want you to take a brownie with you," she said, pointing to the drawer where the plastic wrap was.

"That would be lovely, thank you," I said.

And as I cut a brownie to wrap, she said, "Take more, take two!"

I continued to see Catherine from time to time. Her primary-care nurse happened to be my house mate, Rosie. As a per diem, I cover for the full timers when they are on vacation, sick or have a heavier load. Many patients, though, I have seen more regularly than others because I have requested to visit them or they have asked to see me. Rosie would always have me visit Catherine whenever I was working and each time I visited, I would do Touch on her neck. We often talked about women. Catherine was the fiercely independent type who had never married and though eighty plus years, had been way ahead of her time as a feminist. She definitely preferred female doctors and she loved to hear about accomplished women.

When Catherine's birthday came around, I suggested to Rosie that we take her out for a birthday dinner to Bloodroot, a feminist vegetarian restaurant that I liked very much. Rosie loved the idea and Catherine was thrilled, so we set a date for a "girls night out" birthday celebration.

In her royal blue silk dress, Catherine's blue eyes shined that evening. She moved very slowly using her cane on the stairs to the driveway and her walker on the flat. We parked in the handicapped space as close as we could get to the door and painstakingly she got out of the car and moved into the restaurant. The women at Bloodroot were wonderfully helpful and attentive and we enjoyed our healthful soups, salads and breads, all homemade and tasty. We made sure to try little samples of each other's food so we didn't miss a thing! Catherine, who doesn't usually eat well, ate with such zest, that it was a pleasure to behold, even though it took quite some time. We each had a glass of homemade

May wine and we toasted Catherine and friendship. The owner told us that they infused the wine with Woodruff, and even went outside to pick us some with roots so we could plant some of our own.

For dessert, I had some decadent chocolate cake and Catherine and Rosie had fresh strawberry sundaes. It was quite a feast and quite a night!

You couldn't convince me that a night out wasn't therapeutic. Let's evaluate the benefits by putting it back within the "medical model" (although this was on our "off duty" time): First, it was good for her morale (and ours), second, she got physical therapy, using just about all of her muscle groups: up and down stairs, twice and in and out of the car, twice and to and from the ladies room (quite a hike if you're using a walker), third, it was a very nutritional and healthful meal and her appetite was the best it had ever been (plus she took home a doggie bag for the next day). But that was just for those who may still be in doubt about what a little time, attention and love can do for the health and well-being of another, not to mention what it does for yourself.

When we arrived back at Catherine's, there were hugs and kisses all around. I think her night nurse's aide was ready to call out the Mounties when we arrived at nearly eleven o'clock. Rosie and I had calculated an 8:30 or nine o'clock E.T.A. not figuring on the long walk to the ladies room nor "transfer" time between car and destinations. It was reported that Catherine had her best night's sleep in years and didn't even need to take her usual sleeping pill! Now what better medicine is there?

Chapter 15

Tears, Glorious Tears!

Helen told me that she had been suffering from migraine headaches for the last fifty of her seventy-five years. Today's, she said, she had one of "the bad ones."

Though Touch may not be "within the medical model," many of my colleagues certainly think that it's worth a try when all else has failed. I had been asked by Helen's Primary Care Nurse if I'd go out and do a skilled visit and, "You know," she said in almost a whisper, as I was leaving, "do some of that touch stuff." When one of the other nurses or employees at the agency has a headache or sore shoulders, neck, leg or whatever, I am very often asked to do some Touch and all always say that it helps. When you touch someone, there is always a change.

Helen was a German woman who was very strong and independent for her years. When I arrived, not only did she have a very bad migraine headache, she had neck pain and was nauseated. Though her pain was evident in her tight jaw and strained face, Helen was a stoic woman who did not easily express feelings. I checked her vital signs, and her blood pressure was 160/84, her pulse was 76 and her respirations, 20. I offered her some Touch and she accepted.

Helen sat in a chair and I stood behind her, and, after asking her where it hurt the most, I put my hands on her temples, curving them, as I always do, to fit the contours of where I'm touching. At first, there was no movement under my hands as I met the tension with equal, but gentle pressure. Shortly, I felt some pulsing and I asked Helen what she was noticing. She remarked that she was aware of the pain and a feeling of pulsation. Suddenly she let out a little gasp. "What is it?" I asked.

"I have a terrible pain in my right side," she said, holding her breath.

"Show me where."

She pointed to approximately the gall bladder area and I put my right hand on that place. She put her hand on top of mine and pressed, then started to sob.

"What is it, Helen?" I asked, feeling the tears in my eyes.

"I don't know," she cried, "I never cry and I don't know why I am crying."

"Tears can be sadness," I suggested.

She nodded and continued to cry. I kept my hand on her abdomen and my other arm around her shoulder in a hug. After some time, Helen talked about her husband who had died the year before. She had cared for him at home for almost two years before he died. "I never cried when he was sick and I never cried when he died," she sobbed, "I don't know why I am crying now."

"Do you miss him?"

"I miss him so much." And she cried some more and then started to apologize for crying.

"It's okay to cry. You're grieving the loss of your husband and the life you had together and maybe other losses in your life. Crying is good, it's healthy."

Helen nodded and, reaching into her pocket to pull out a tissue, wiped her tears and blew her nose. She took a big breath and sighed, then she put her face in her hands and cried some more. I stood silently with my arms around her.

When someone has trusted me enough to cry in my presence, I never console. I never stick a box of tissues under the nose of a person who is crying (they have to ask for a tissue, first.) These reactions, though well intentioned, are really giving that person a message to not cry. A pat on the back can give the message, "There, there, don't cry, everything will be alright..." a tissue pushed into that person's hand can be saying, "Here, blow your nose and be quiet."

At first it's difficult being with a person that is crying. We can feel helpless, like we have to do something or make it better. Well, the best thing we can do is to just acknowledge that tears are okay and just be present and really hear their pain.

Profound loneliness is one thing that has been expressed to me often by many patients. Especially after the loss of a lifelong companion, their days and nights can be torturously long and often frightening. I am convinced that people do die of broken hearts and loneliness, though the medical examiner's report will state something a little more technical. In spite of Senior Centers and support groups for widows and widowers, many older people don't drive or are afraid to go out of their homes. Most home care agencies or city and town social agencies have volunteers who will visit patients, though some patients feel uncomfortable with "strangers" or are afraid they are "too much trouble" and don't want to "bother" anyone. More often than not, they will express frustration at not feeling productive or useful anymore.

Everyone needs to be heard. We may listen, but do we really hear? People may talk, but do we hear the feelings behind the words? If someone constantly is complaining what is the feeling? Are they angry or scared? If we really hear someone, we will try to understand the feeling behind the words and validate that feeling.

We all need to be seen. When we are with someone, do we really see them? Do we look them in the eyes, do we notice how they move, how they breathe? Do they look comfortable, tense or agitated? Do we see their beautiful, sparkling eyes, their warm smile, their handmade quilt or lovely flower garden? Their home reflects a lot about them, is it open and light or cluttered and dark?

All of us need to be touched. With another's permission, touching can be a hug, a touch or holding of a hand, or gentle hands on an area of tension or pain. Touching is the physical affirmation that we do indeed really hear and see that person who is before us. Whenever we touch someone, we have made a difference.

When Helen had finished crying, she glanced around and asked me for another tissue, which was out of her reach. We hugged and she thanked me, saying that her headache was completely gone and that she had no pain anywhere!

Before I left, I took her vital signs again. Just for the record, they had settled down nicely to 140/70 - pulse 64 and respirations 18!

Chapter 16

Something in French

Having been born and raised in Paris, Nicole's first language was French. When we first met, she was in her early forties, married with two children and had no recollection at all of her native language, though her brother and sisters still spoke it fluently.

As a member of an experiential therapy group that I facilitated, Nicole had come because of marital difficulties and general unhappiness. She had been diagnosed with Lupus, as had her older brother, an illness that her mother had died of. She was weak, sleeping often, had skin blotches and was losing handfuls of her dark hair. A pretty woman, Nicole was shapely and feminine and had a wonderful smile, though she didn't smile often. Most of the time, she sat fearfully on the side-lines and didn't speak much or participate in many of the experiential exercises. What she was most afraid of was Touch, though that was also what had attracted her to the group in the first place.

After about six months, Nicole finally began opening up, and we learned that her father had been physically abusive, regularly beating Nicole's mother and brother. She had also remembered being beaten with a strap and a time, when she was sixteen, when her father punched her in the face and broke her glasses. She said she would wear long-sleeved sweaters, even in the summer, to conceal the welts and bruises. Another punishment was the withholding of food. She had no memory of any other childhood events, only those after the age of fourteen or fifteen years old.

Over the next two months, Nicole shared with the group more and more. She spoke about her abusive husband, whom she had been with for twenty years but could not seem to leave. She smiled more and even laughed with us, but she never cried.

One evening, Nicole finally agreed to lie on the table for a Touch session, in the presence of the small group of women she had come to know intimately over the previous eight months.

She had indicated that an area that she was very much aware of was her upper chest, just below her throat. Placing one hand gently in that area, I put the other one on her shoulder. Nicole lay, with her eyes wide open, and held her breath, before beginning to take some cautious, shallow breaths. We were all silent for some time, as her breathing increased and I could feel her heart's pounding vibrating her chest.

"Nicole," I said softly, but her body jumped in alarm, "Your heart is pounding and your breathing is very fast, are you aware of that?"

"No."

"Well, see if you can feel that," I suggested.

She closed her eyes momentarily, then opened them suddenly. "I feel it," she said.

"What does that feel like to you?"

"I don't know. What do you think it is?"

"It feels like it might be fear. Are you afraid?"

"I don't know," she whispered, then closed her eyes again, "Yes, I am afraid."

"See if you can just be with that fear, then."

She kept her eyes closed and the lids fluttered. Her breathing increased, so she was almost gasping and then she began to speak rapidly and urgently in French!

After a few minutes, I asked her what was happening.

"It's Papa," she said, "He's got no clothes on and he's in my bed and he's hurting me!"

"How old are you?"

"I'm six," she said and she began to cry.

"How do you feel about that six year old?"

"I hate her! She is ugly and bad!"

"Who tells her that?"

"Papa tells me that if I were a good girl, he wouldn't have to hurt me."

"Nicole, just for a moment, see if you can really look at her. Really look at her and tell me what you see?"

"She is very small, and scared."

"And what does she do when Papa is hurting her?"

"She blanks out, leaves her body." Nicole opened her eyes, suddenly, tears streaming down her cheeks and whispered, "That's what I do all of the time, 'blank out'!"

"Close your eyes for just another moment," I asked her, "and see that little six year old Nicole. Can you thank her for making it possible for you to survive that terrible abuse without going insane?"

She closed her eyes again and nodded. Then she began to sob.

"Nicole, you are safe now, but I know how much it hurts." I felt the tears burn my eyes as I felt anger about the excruciating pain a father can inflict with his abuse of power. But my tears were also those of joy, for though Nicole was going through overwhelming pain, I knew that she was getting what she needed to continue her journey and her healing.

As children of abuse and incest, we have no choices. We are victims and so we have to block out painful memories to survive. Once we become adults, we may spend many years making unconscious choices to create our present life so it can match or validate our stored feelings, giving us a reason to keep them hidden. It is only when we feel safe enough, accepted enough and loved enough that we can allow ourselves to be vulnerable and finally reexperience the painful memories and traumatic feelings on a conscious level.

One of the most damaging feelings that I had from my incest experience was that it was my fault, that I was responsible. Well, as a child, I was not, but as an adult, if I continue to allow myself to be abused, physically, emotionally, psychologically or spiritually, then indeed, I have chosen to remain a victim. The tricky part comes in becoming conscious as an adult, to those self-defeating and self-destructive behaviors that have become so much a part of us. Here is where the difference is, with Touch: rather than trying to "get rid of" the self-destructive behavior, we are able to "be with it" instead. We embrace it, we thank it for making it possible to survive our lives thus far, rather than banishing it, like an abused child.

Loving ourselves, every part, is a painful, wonderful and necessary part of healing our bodies, minds and spirits.

Nicole eventually left her husband and is taking care of herself more and more each day. Her Lupus is in remission, she has more energy and she smiles, laughs and cries. She has become more outgoing and has lost much of her fear and tries new things each day. She called me recently, thrilled and triumphant that she had actually gone skiing for the first time and loved it.

"I did well, I couldn't believe it. I never thought I'd have the strength or coordination, but I did it! I was afraid at first, but I just felt the fear, then I did it anyway!"

A lot of grieving to do

Monica, a woman who had been sexually molested as a child by her father and brothers, was referred to me for eight sessions by her therapist. For forty-five to fifty minutes of every session that I saw her, she would lie on the table, my hands on her, and cry. Most of the time it was a very quiet sobbing, sometimes her body would quietly shake and shudder with deep sobs. She would always soak the sheet on the table around her face so I used to put several towels underneath for each session and never gave her a tissue unless she asked (which she didn't do until the end of the session). Too often, our programmed and seemingly well-intentioned response to tears is to give that person a tissue. If we're honest with ourselves, this non-verbal message may be: "Dry your tears and stop crying because it is making me uncomfortable." Monica had a lot of grieving to do for her lost innocence and childhood and crying was what she needed to do. The Touch sessions allowed her to move through much of the grief to free her up to continue with her therapist. We have to be with those old stored feelings first, before we can move through them. She moved to Oregon and is now living that life she always dreamed of, doing those things that she loves to do. Imagine what would have happened if, when she started crying, she was automatically handed a tissue.

Chapter 17

When Healing Is Letting Go

One evening while working at a Convalescent Home, I got a call on my office phone. It was an outside line, but the call was from Frank, a patient on the second floor who had a phone in his room. This, I thought was a very creative way to bypass the nurse's station, thus cutting out the middle-man.

"This is the Nursing Supervisor, isn't it?" his gruff voice asked.

"Yes, what can I do for you, Mr. Cassidy?"

"Well, I've been ringing and ringing for the nurse, but she won't come. They're ignoring me and I'm in pain."

"I'll check into it," I promised.

After calling the nurse on his floor and being told that she had already medicated him for pain and that she couldn't give him anything more for three hours, I went to visit him. Frank Cassidy sat with his bed cranked in the full upright position that most people with emphysema find the easiest position to breathe in. He was a small, white-haired man in his early eighties and for a moment I stood at his opened door, watching him struggle for air. Noting that his respirations were 32, I knocked and entered after he asked me to come in.

"My name is Linda, Mr. Cassidy, may I call you Frank?"

"Yes, of course," he said as he motioned for me to sit down.

"You told me on the phone that you're in pain. Where is your pain?" I asked as I pulled the chair closer to the bed and sat down.

"Right here," he replied, pointing to his diaphragm area that was retracting with each difficult inhalation.

"May I touch you where it hurts?"

Frank nodded and I placed my hands gently over his heaving diaphragm and let them follow his breaths. A few moments later he closed his eyes and spoke softly, "When I was a boy, I used to go with my mother to the homes of sick people. There was always a group of others there, too and they did the 'laying on of hands'."

"Did it work?" I asked.

"Oh yes," he said emphatically, opening his eyes momentarily, before closing them again with a sigh. I noticed his respirations had slowed a little, he was breathing more easily. We sat in silence for some time, my hands quietly in place, before he said, "You know, my lovely wife, Esther, died four years ago and I just haven't been the same since. Most all of my friends are gone now, too."

"It sounds like there's been a lot of pain in your life," I said softly, my hands remaining in gentle contact with him.

"Yes...there has," he whispered as tears emerged from the corners of his still closed eyes. "I'm ready to go now too. I'm ready to be with Esther again."

"You must be tired, Frank. Ready to move on."

"Yes," he smiled, opening his eyes with another deep sigh, "Yes, I am very tired." His respirations were down to 24 and his color was better. "The pain is gone and I think that I could sleep, now."

Keeping my hands gently on him, we sat a while longer, before I slowly removed them. "Just call if you want me to come back again," I whispered. He smiled, nodded and closed his eyes.

Twenty minutes later, I got a stat call from the floor nurse: Frank was in respiratory distress and was being taken to the hospital. I ran down the stairs and caught Frank as he was being taken out to the ambulance on a stretcher:

When he saw me, he smiled and opened his arms. We hugged. "Thank you," he whispered.

"I'll never forget you, Frank," I said. Tears burned my eyes.

"Or I, you." He smiled and they took him off to the hospital.

I was not at all surprised when an hour later an ER nurse called to tell me that Frank had died. I cried tears of joy, not only for Frank, but for myself. It had never occurred to me until then, that death could be a healing. Twenty years before, when my mother had died of breast cancer at the age of forty-eight, I was so wrapped up in my own grief that I couldn't even fathom that perhaps death was a healing for her. I had spent many years unaware that I was holding on to the anger of losing her when I was so young until Frank died. In that moment, I felt such relief: it was as if I finally knew that Mom was alright and was where she needed to be. Peace about Mom was the gift that Frank gave to me.

Chapter 18

A Very Deep Hurt

She lived in Florida most of the year, but came back to her home in Connecticut for several weeks around the Holidays. Eleanor, in her late eighties, was small, spry, and moved quickly with purpose. Reserved and quiet, she arrived for her first session of Touch dressed warmly in black boots, mittens and a knit hat pulled over her gray hair.

We talked for some time, getting her background and medical history. She had a left mastectomy twenty years before with no further problems. A year ago she had begun to have increasing pain and most recently, ulceration of the skin in the operative area.

Because it would have been uncomfortable for her to lie face down on the table, the session began with Eleanor lying on her back and draped. As I examined the mastectomy site, I found it to be red with several ulcerated areas that were blistered and full of a clear yellow fluid. There was a bandage over another ulcerated area that had opened and was draining. Her ulcerated chest and the odor of cancer brought those feelings about my mother's illness and death back vividly. I took a breath. I know that many people think that the sight of blood, trauma and the ravages of disease don't bother nurses and doctors and other health care professionals. That's not so, and we all have different ways of coping. I remind myself that though a patient may have a disease, they are not that disease. Though the body may not always appear beautiful at first, once we can acknowledge and then get beyond the body, true beauty lies in the spirit of that person. Marion Rosen once said that we all need to be listened to, looked at and touched. That need, I believe, is never so great as when we are sick or in pain physically, emotionally or spiritually. Looking at Eleanor that first day, so reminded me of my mother and brought up old fears, that I didn't want to touch her ulcerated chest. I also knew that that was where my hands needed to be. She lay quietly on the table, her eyes closed. Before touching her, I closed my eyes and felt my fear and silently told myself that it was okay to be afraid. Then I took a breath, lay my hands on her ulcerated chest and gave Eleanor my complete attention. The fear left me.

Under my hands, I felt the superficial softness of the ulcers, then a hardness and a stillness in her chest. Though I make patients aware of what I am noticing and ask them to tell me what they may be feeling, I tell them that they need not talk. I only ask that they are aware of the changes and what they may be experiencing.

My hands quietly in place and focusing on Eleanor, I thought about cancer as Mom described it as being anger turned inward and felt that to be a very deep hurt.

"Cancer can be a very deep hurt," I offered softly.

There was a tightening in her chest and momentarily she held her breath. Then she sighed, "I can't believe it but it's true...and after all of these years..." Under my hands came a small vibration and then a trembling, her chest heaved and Eleanor began to softly sob. She continued crying for most of the rest of our time together and said nothing more. From time to time I would tell her that I was noticing a change in her body, she would occasionally nod, eyes remaining closed. When the session was over, she made an appointment for the following week, thanked me and left.

I saw Eleanor once a week for the next two weeks she was in Connecticut and three more times the following year at Holiday time. With each session there was a subtle change that I noticed, an opening, a softening under my hands, as she cried quietly on the table, though there was very little verbal communication. Then, after each session, Eleanor would prefer to shake hands because she said that she didn't know how to hug comfortably.

Being reserved and quite stoic, I believe that tears shed in the presence of another was a rarity for her. I felt both grateful and honored to have been a witness. I never knew the circumstances around her deep hurt so many years before, but that didn't matter because I was not there to analyze, only to be present. If she had chosen to tell me, that would have been fine. Sometimes a patient isn't consciously aware of the circumstances, either. Only an awareness of what is, and acceptance of that by the patient and practitioner, are all that are needed to create an environment for healing.

The last time I saw Eleanor, she had again, cried quietly on the table for most of the session. "I will be going back to Florida tomorrow," she said, as she put on her knit, wool hat. "I wonder if it would be alright if we hugged good-bye today."

I always love to hug my patients so I said with a smile, "I thought you'd never ask!"

After we hugged, Eleanor said thank you and turned to go. She stopped and turned back towards me, "Thank you, again, for everything," she paused, seemingly uncomfortable, then added softly, "Thank you for the love. Because you know, that's what it is...love."

She left in a quiet dusting of Connecticut snow and I never saw her again.

Chapter 19

Whatever It Is In Sam Hill...

Rita lived alone, had COPD (chronic obstructive pulmonary disease) was on continuous oxygen and was prone to what she called "panic attacks." She not only took all kinds of medicine prescribed for her by umpteen different doctors for her ailment as well as for her anxiety, but she would often abuse alcohol.

Whenever I visited Rita, she would talk incessantly about how her family, friends, doctors, tenants and anyone else available, had abandoned and neglected her. She adored her father, who died "when I needed him the most," one month after her thirteenth birthday. Rita, now in her early seventies, though looking younger because she colored her hair and palpable rage gives off a lot of energy, was still grieving his loss.

Having spent many hours with my hands on Rita as she reexperienced her pain, living in the shadows of her past rage, I also have seen a terrified little child emerge. At those times, Rita has softened and opened to reveal that lovable part that she works so hard to conceal.

The first time I did Touch on Rita, she was having one of her "panic attacks" and so, after asking if it were okay to touch her, I gently placed my hands on her shoulders, where she said she felt the most tension, then asked her to describe what it felt like when she had an attack.

"Well, I get this fluttery feeling in my stomach, then I break out into a cold sweat, then suddenly I feel like I can't breathe and my chest and shoulders get tense and hurt and then I feel like I want to scream and sometimes I do...." Then she was quiet for a few minutes and on the verge of tears asked, "Why do you think I get these panic attacks?"

"Are you afraid?" I asked.

"You're damn right I'm afraid!" she answered in her usual "tough guy" way.

"Do you want to talk about that fear?"

"No, not now, I just want to feel your hands on me," she said, closing her eyes with a sigh.

We were silent for some time and, as I held my hands on her, I could feel her rapid breathing become deeper and slower. There was softening under my hands and then came some pulsating.

"Rita," I said softly, "What are you noticing?"

She took in a deep breath, her shoulders dropped some more, "Well," she said, "whatever it is in Sam Hill that you're doing...it's working!"

CHAPTER 20

WHEN SOMEONE CARES

Lenny and Maggie lived in the trailer park, their baby blue mobile home surrounded with pinwheels, a flamingo and other brightly colored lawn ornaments. Maggie, missing several teeth, always had a warm smile and hearty laugh to welcome me and applied her make-up as colorfully as she had decorated the outside of the trailer. In her late seventies with poor eyesight, she had thin-penciled eyebrows that were often lopsided, where she has drawn one, eyebrows down, the other, eyebrows up, giving her a half startled look. She had a bawdy voice and a Cockney accent which I loved, and though I'd heard it several times, never got tired of her story of how she and Lenny met.

"Oh, Lenny was handsome back then, ee was, ee's thin now, but you should have seen him then!" she began, grinning over at Lenny, who sat quietly on the couch. He was hunched forward, breathing rapidly, as he always did. "Me mates and I were walking along and here comes this beautiful, shiny car, the kind with the convertible top, ya know, and it's Lenny and his friend. I said to my friends, 'Oh, would I love to have a ride in that car.' And sure enough, Lenny and his friend come back and ask us if we want a ride. Well, me mates don't think we should but I say 'Aw, come on, girls!' and I finally convince em to get in. At first I was interested in Lenny's friend because it was his car." Here, Maggie winked over at Lenny, who smiled. "But I wasn't blind and it didn't take me long to see who was the nicest guy, not to mention the most handsome!" She laughed loudly. "We've been together almost fifty years, now, eh Lenny, love?"

Lenny nodded, as he took in a deep breath between his rapid short ones. Having constant angina (heart) pain, Lenny always told me that he was afraid of becoming addicted to the pain medication that the doctor prescribed. Instead he used his oxygen most of the time, which helped to keep the pain under control.

Lenny sat on the couch with no oxygen on, explaining that he liked to go without it for a little while a couple of times each day. Behind the couch was Lenny's work bench, with hundreds of little drawers and tools, wires and other mysterious stuff. Lenny was a Ham Radio operator, and had managed to pack the radio equipment and all of the radio repair tools and supplies neatly into the little trailer.

"Lenny is a master at it!" Maggie piped up, proudly, "Everyone used to bring things for him to fix. Not just radio stuff, either. Lenny can fix anything electronic or mechanical. Ee's a genius!"

"Oh, Maggie, you make it sound so important. Besides, I can't do it anymore, I just get too tired," Lenny said quietly.

"It is important and you still do some repairs, ya know!"

"I'm impressed, Lenny," I said, "Would you tell me about your Ham Radio?"

Lenny explained how it worked and demonstrated by connecting briefly to someone in Germany. "I have friends all over the world that I've been talking to for years," Lenny added. He showed me electronic circuit boards, many that he had designed and built himself.

As a gentle, quiet man and a man of few words, Lenny rarely complained. On that day, after I examined him, checked his vital signs, assessed his condition and reviewed his medications, I asked him about the pain he was having at that time.

"It's pretty bad right now," he admitted.

"What about when you have the oxygen on?"

"If I lie down and wear the oxygen, it's usually better, but I don't want to lie in bed all day long."

"I do a little hands on work," I said, "may I touch you where you have the pain?"

He agreed and I asked him to show me specifically where the pain was. Lenny pointed to his sternum area, just above his diaphragm, so I gently placed my hand there as it retracted sharply with each rapid inhalation. He sat in a hunched position, shoulders up and rounded forward and visibly held tension in his neck, jaw and pale face. Very tall and thin, Lenny's clavicle and scapular bones protruded sharply through his worn t-shirt. He was unshaven, wore thick, black-rimmed glasses, but his sparse, gray hair was neatly combed.

When I asked him to describe the pain, he told me it was sharp at first, then would ache terribly for awhile, then it would become sharp again. "Sometimes it feels like a squeezing in my chest and then I have more trouble breathing than usual."

"Are you having trouble breathing now?"

"Well, no, but I notice that I'm taking little breaths. It's almost like I'm waiting for the pain to get sharp again, like it always does..."

"Is the pain constant?"

"Pretty much, but not all of the time."

"It's all of the time!" Maggie said loudly, "Don't listen to him! And I worry somethin' terrible about him!"

"Well, yes, pretty much," conceded Lenny, with a sigh.

"It must be terrible to be in constant pain," I said.

"It's not fun."

I kept my hand on his diaphragm area, following his body as it breathed laboriously, the other hand, quietly on his shoulder. He spoke some more about his physical pain and expressed frustration at being unable to do those things he enjoyed doing. "I really don't want to go on living like this."

"Aw, will you stop talkin like that, Lenny!" Maggie said, waving her hand at him. "Ya know it upsets me when ya say that!"

"Are you saying that you're tired of living in pain all of the time?" I asked.

"Yes," Lenny sighed softly. I could feel some softening under both of my hands and his breathing was a little slower. He closed his eyes for awhile as I continued to keep my hands in gentle contact. We sat in silence for perhaps another ten minutes before he opened his eyes and said that he wanted to go and lie down.

He stood up slowly and shuffled off toward the bedroom but after a few steps, turned to face me and said, "You may not think that what you do makes a difference, but it does. Some of these nurses rush in and take my blood pressure, then rush out. But you really care. When someone cares, it really makes a difference...." Then he turned and quietly left the room.

CHAPTER 21

CHARLIE'S CHALLENGE

Charlie wanted to have Touch sessions because, he said, he felt stressed out and tense almost all of the time. He was a small, wiry man, in his mid fifties who had been divorced once and widowed once, with four grown children. His oldest son had been killed in a car accident fifteen years before. He had a deep, raspy voice, dark intense eyes and wore his black hair combed slickly away from his tanned, lined face.

"I have never cried in my life," he said at his first session, before he even lay on the table.

"Is there any reason you are telling me that?" I asked.

"No, no reason, why?"

"It almost sounds like a challenge. Is it?"

He thought for a moment. "Well, maybe it is," he smiled, "But it will never happen. I didn't even cry when my mother died, or my wife. I thought I would when my son was killed, but I didn't...."

"Before we start," I said softly, "I just want you to know that the purpose of this work is not to make you cry or laugh or even to make you relax. It's only about being with what is. If you don't cry, that's fine. One thing I do know is that you will get whatever you need."

Coming for sessions once a week for almost six months, Charlie revealed himself, his body softening, his face relaxing, as a man filled with much sadness and pain. From his earliest recollections, he had many losses, all which he seemed to bear bravely and alone. As the oldest son he became the "man of the house" when he was seven after his father died suddenly. A private man, Charlie rarely acknowledged his feelings to anyone, least of all, himself. When he was feeling vulnerable or tender, he would usually make a joke. He had spoken often about his intense need to be held and how he had translated that into sex, having had many unfulfilling sexual relationships.

"I think what every man really wants is to get back into the womb," he had said once, "and sex is the next best thing."

The last time I saw Charlie, he lay on his back on the table, and was speaking about the loss of his son and how it touched that part of himself that he had lost at such a young age. I asked him where he felt that pain and he pointed to his chest, over his heart. Moving my hands to that place, I asked him to describe the physical feeling he was having there.

"It's a tightness, almost suffocating feeling. It's overwhelming pain...."

And I knew that he was feeling deeply and was completely present. My eyes burned with tears, his chest softened, then got tight again momentarily before I felt a vibration, then it trembled under my hands. Charlie's eyes shut tighter, his whole face working to keep them closed and he was swallowing frequently and hard.

"What are you noticing, Charlie?" I whispered.

He did not answer, but sighed deeply, before tears squeezed out from the sides of his eyes and his chin quivered. His whole body seemed to be working desperately to hide his grief.

"Charlie, do you want me to stay with you or would you like to be alone?" I asked.

"Alone," he managed to whisper.

I slowly removed my hands, covered him with the sheet, telling him that if he wanted me to come back, he had only to call and quietly left the room. As soon as I had closed the door behind me, I heard a sob and then muffled wails, that continued for quite some time. After about a half hour, Charlie emerged from the room, neatly dressed. His face was swollen and his eyes, reddened, but he smiled from a face that, in spite of the swelling, looked ten years younger.

"How do you feel?" I asked.

"A little foolish, but wonderful," he said with a big sigh.

"You sound relieved."

"I am. Very. You were right. I got what I needed."

We hugged good-bye and that was the last time I saw Charlie.

CHAPTER 22

JUST FOR THE RECORD

Having lived for years with emphysema, Robin, a woman in her sixties, said she wished that she had never even seen a cigarette. She pushed a walker with wheels, trailing yards of green oxygen tubing behind her wherever she went in her house. Even walking from one room to another would leave her panting for breath and she would find taking a shower exhausting.

When Robin and I first talked, she said she believed that touch was terribly important and was very willing to try a Touch session. Of course, I had checked her vital signs and done my other nurse stuff, but then I had her lie down across her bed on her back. For Robin, lying on her back didn't seem to be a problem, unlike others I have known with the same illness. Her neck, shoulders and of course chest muscles (from her labored breathing) were the areas that she found painful. I had also decided to check her vital signs after she had been Touched. Though I am convinced that Touch is always helpful in some way, I thought perhaps "before and after" vital signs would be some nice statistics, just for the record.

Before she had fifteen minutes of Touch, her blood pressure was 120/62, her pulse was 96 and her respirations were 24. All were taken when Robin was at rest and had been at rest for a good twenty minutes.

After the Touch session, Robin said that the pain in her chest, shoulders and neck was gone, and she remarked that she was able to breathe through her nose only, something that she was never able to do. Her blood pressure was down to 100/60, her pulse at a nice 80 beats per minute and her respirations were at a remarkable 16! On my next visit, her vital signs, at rest, before the Touch session were 122/80 - 88 -24 and after, they were 110/70 - 80 -16.

For about a year and a half, I saw Robin once or twice a week and we became very close. One of the many wonderful benefits of Touch is that, in a very short time, there is an incredible amount of trust that develops. I remember a patient that came for Touch sessions early in my private practice. A man in his fifties, who, after his first session remarked, "I can't believe I told you what I did. I have never told those things to anyone before!"

Because of her illness, Robin was very susceptible to flu and other lung problems so she had frequent lung infections that needed to be treated with antibiotics. At these times, she would jokingly ask me to "beat her."

This was called chest P.T. or chest percussion and it's a great old stand-by using vibration and gravity. Robin would hang over the side of her bed, and I would percuss her back over her lungs with cupped hands. I've also heard it called "cupping" or "clapping." That's what it sounds like, but what it does is loosen the secretions in the lungs so they can be coughed up, helping to clear the lungs of someone who otherwise has great difficulty doing so.

We would alternate Touch with "beatings" when she needed them, and Robin would always let me know what she needed. We are both convinced that some of those lung infections she had would have landed her in the hospital if not for the Touch, and the "beatings."

Robin once said, "If I could have Touch three or four times a week, I could probably get rid of 99% of my pills and I take a lot of pills."

She also talked about her panic attacks, "I don't think it's right that I get panic attacks, I really have nothing to get so anxious about..." (though I think it must be very frightening to be so short of breath) "...but when I get them, I am so tense, it just isn't funny and I gasp for breath. This Touch, no massage or anything, just Touch, makes them go away, even thinking about being touched makes them start to go away."

It was Robin who arranged for me to speak about Touch for her "Better Breathing Club," which is coordinated by the American Lung Association. It is a group of men and women with a variety of lung diseases who meet once a week for support, sharing, information and education. They were a very enthusiastic and vital group of people who were open and receptive to the benefits of Touch. It was quite an honor to have been invited to be there with them.

It was sometime after that first year and a half that I had been seeing Robin that she went into the hospital with congestive heart failure and was put in the intensive care unit on a respirator. When I was able to visit her, she could not speak because the respirator tubing was connected to a tracheotomy, a hole directly into her "wind pipe.". When I walked in the room and she saw me, she beamed and opened her arms wide for a big hug. We struggled to communicate, Robin writing out what she was trying to say, but having difficulty because of the IV in her right hand.

Her nurse had told me that they had been working on weaning Robin off of the respirator for about an hour twice a day, and that she would sit in a panic and watch the clock tick away each minute of the hour that she had to breathe on her own. While I was visiting, they planned on taking her off for an hour, so I asked Robin if I could do some Touch while she was off of the respirator. She smiled and nodded.

The first thing I noticed, of course, was a huge wall clock that was facing Robin's bed. Now I know that a clock is needed in each ICU room, but perhaps behind the patient's bed, where the patient can't see it, would be a better spot.

When the respirator was removed and her tracheotomy plugged, Robin looked panicked. She was hooked up to monitors and so there, suspended above her bed, was the monitor screen where I could read her ever changing vital signs that were being continuously recorded.

I placed my hand softly on her chest as it panted in rapid, shallow breaths. Her vital signs were high, reflecting her anxiety and difficulty breathing and of course the oxygen saturation percentage in her blood was low. She kept mouthing the question, "How long? An hour?" fairly frequently for the first ten minutes or so, but soon, closed her eyes as her vital signs slowly made their descent into a more normal range and her O2 saturation increased. It was quite a wonderful sight: Robin, eyes closed, face relaxed, color better. Feeling her chest under my hands as each breath became less labored and for that scientific side of me, being able to occasionally glance up at the monitor and have what I was feeling, with my hands and with my heart, confirmed, was very exciting.

Robin was transferred to a rehabilitation facility for several weeks where she continued to work on being weaned off of the respirator during the day. A doctor there had told her that she would have to use the respirator all night at home for the rest of her life and so would always have her tracheotomy.

That doctor didn't know Robin. She has impressive determination, tenacity and heart. At first, she was frightened to be back home, though her husband, Dennis gives her wonderful care. But Robin is very independent and it didn't take her long before she was doing most everything for herself again. It was only a few weeks after she was home from rehab that I was out to lunch with some friends and looked over and, lo and behold, there's Robin, portable oxygen, trach and all having lunch with Dennis! She is quite an inspiration. I am proud to say that Robin made a liar out of that doctor: she doesn't use the respirator at all and her tracheotomy tube was removed last week!

Chapter 23

Opening Day

Doc lived in a small silver trailer and sat in his usual chair at the tiny formica kitchen table. A cigar was always in a nearby ashtray, though rarely lit. He was surrounded by piles of old newspapers and hundreds of cigar boxes filled with keepsakes he'd collected and fishing flies that he'd tied over most of his eighty-six years. His ears stuck out a bit, and a boyish grin always filled the trailer when I came in the door. It was that kind of smile that made you think that it was smiled just for you.

In his younger days, he'd been a deer hunter and there were several pair of antlers on the walls and in a corner or two, but his pride and joy was fishing and tying flies. He'd even created some of his own, which he proudly showed me along with the boxes and boxes of neutral to brightly colored flies of all sizes. Doc explained which flies were used, depending on what time of year it was and what kind of fish you wanted to catch.

Doc was visited once or twice a month for a general health assessment and, each time I saw him, I learned more about fishing. Having done some fly fishing myself, I really enjoyed Doc's fish stories and even had some of my own to tell. Since the first time his father had taken him fishing as a little boy, he had never missed an opening day. As a grown man, though he had no children of his own, Doc volunteered every year at the state park and local boy scouts to teach his skill and love of fishing and fly tying.

His wife had died many years before and when he spoke of her, his eyes always filled with tears. His only family was a nephew who visited occasionally. I never left his little trailer without a bagful of frozen trout or "catch of the day" and some clams or mussels.

It was in the spring that Doc took a turn for the worse. I went to visit him one evening because he had not been feeling well, but didn't want to go to the doctor. He had lost his appetite and was weak and I did not find him in his usual chair, but rather curled up in his bed which filled the entire bedroom of the trailer. He was fully dressed but had wet himself, though he was unaware that he had. I washed him and helped him change his clothes. His lungs were congested, his heart rate rapid and irregular and he was having great difficulty breathing.

"Doc, I'd like to send you to the hospital so they can check you out," I said.

"No, I don't want to go," he said weakly, "I just want to rest here, in my home."

"I'll call your doctor anyway, and let him know how you are and that you want to stay here. How about I call your nephew and see if he'll come down and stay with you tonight?"

"You can call the doctor, but don't bother my nephew."

After I called Dr. Bradley, I came back and sat on the bed next to Doc. He told me that his chest was sore and I asked if I could Touch him where it hurt. He agreed. We sat in silence, my hand gently on his chest, as it moved rapidly and with great effort. I knew he was dying and that a trip to the hospital was not in his plan. Doc had been getting progressively weaker and weaker the last few months, with some dizzy spells and unsteadiness. He had not been able to drive and had lost his independence, having to rely on his nephew, neighbors or friends.

"I've had a good life," Doc smiled weakly.

"Doc, you're a good man and so many people love you. I love you." I said, kissing his rough cheek.

He grinned once more, that big boyish grin of his, "You make me happy."

"I love your smile. You make me happy, too," I whispered.

I saw a tear roll back onto his pillow and felt one on my face.

Not wanting him to be alone overnight, I asked him once more if I could call his nephew. He finally agreed. When I spoke with Alan, he, of course, wanted to be with his uncle and said he'd be there in an hour.

"What do I do if he gets worse?" Alan asked.

"Well, you could offer to call 9-1-1, but if he doesn't want you to, just keep him comfortable and be with him."

"Do you think he's dying?"

"Yes, I do," I said softly, "I'm sure you know that he's been very weak lately and that he's never missed an opening day for fishing yet. It's sometime soon, isn't it?"

"Oh," Alan said, "Opening day is Saturday."

"It is?" I asked, thinking this was Thursday, and suddenly it all fell into place.

Alan spent that night with his uncle and the next day, Doc became unresponsive. Doc never regained consciousness and died on Friday night.

I'm sure that my mother, patients and all those I have loved who have died are where they need to be. My scientific mind tells me that they have died with their bodies but my heart doesn't believe that. I've learned from my patients that death is a natural part of life and that, though those of us who are living may fear it because we think it will be a painful struggle, it's actually easier than we think. Painful times in my life were actually times of transition, though during those times I was unaware of that fact. I could never see what possible good could have come out of them but, looking back, they were all a necessary and wonderful part of my journey. My patients have shown me that death is a transition. Sometimes, when I am on a plane, I look out at the clouds and imagine my mother sitting all "soft and fluffy" on one, smiling her love on me. Sometimes, I have felt her near me when I have been alone. One day, the little stuffed lamb I keep on my bed, with a music box in it that plays one of her favorite hymns, spontaneously began to play. Without hesitation I said, "Hello, Mom."

With Mom, and others that I love, I can only imagine where their spirits may be, but with Doc, I am sure.

He died on Friday because he had never missed an opening day in his life since that day, so many years before, when his father had first taken him fishing. Now I don't know if there's a river in heaven, or even if there is a heaven, but whenever I've been on a river fishing, it certainly has felt like heaven to me. Doc touched many lives, sharing with them his knowledge and love of fishing. Undoubtedly, many of them and their children and even grandchildren, were up bright and early on that Saturday morning casting their lines into the water...

Doc did make opening day, after all, and it seems to me he always will...

Chapter 24

"I Had To Tell You First..."

Pregnant with her second child, Amy had six weeks to go until her due date. She called for an appointment because she was very upset and wanted to come the the office right away. Having had her first child delivered by a midwife when she had lived in New York City, Amy had not liked the way she had been treated by the group of obstetric doctors who had been following her pregnancy, "I feel like a piece of meat," she had said, "I hardly ever see my doctor, or even the same doctor and I feel rushed and unimportant."

When she arrived for the session, we hugged and she started to cry.

"What is it? What's been happening?" I asked her.

"Well, my doctor told me yesterday that I will probably have to have a Caesarean Section because the baby is in a breech position," she sobbed. "He says that there is only a slim chance that the baby will turn because it's so big and I'm so close to my due date that there's no room for it to turn. He told me to prepare myself for a Caesarean Section... and I so wanted to have another natural birth like I did with Julie."

I had her lie on her side for the session and gently placed my hands on her abdomen, particularly her diaphragm area, which was very tight. Amy told me her feelings about the new baby's arrival, how her three year old had been acting out and some concerns about her mother-in-law. She felt criticized and that, try as she did, to do what she felt was her best, it never felt like it was good enough. There were some feelings of being out of control of her body, like she was being carried along by her pregnancy, almost a feeling of being possessed by an alien.

"I have such ambivalence," she said, "I know it sounds terrible, but I can't wait until this baby is out of me!"

"I don't think that sounds terrible. It's certainly understandable. When I was pregnant with Meagan, I couldn't wait to have my body back!" We laughed at how newborns, as beautiful as they are, often look like little aliens when they're brand new.

Amy expressed frustration in her lack of energy and thought her husband could help out more with their daughter. He had been very busy on a big project and hadn't had much time for his family. Working in his studio at home, he would shut himself away and their little girl didn't understand.

Being very pregnant as she was, she felt that she wasn't attractive to her husband and his increase in work and spending less time with his wife and child, only seemed to confirm her worries. Though Amy knew he was a loving husband and father, she needed more reassurance at that time.

She felt that though it was unspoken, her mother-in-law didn't like her, nor did she approve of how she was raising her granddaughter or how she was "taking care of" her son. Amy also referred to little insinuations and digs about her housekeeping and cooking and felt like her mother-in-law was trying to alienate her husband from her.

Throughout the session, I kept my hands quietly in place, meeting the tension that I felt underneath them but not trying to force a change. Relaxation can't be forced and often, the opposite is true. The more we try to change, the more tense we become and get stuck in the trying rather than to relax into what is, into the being.

An old story I once heard about a contest between the sun and the wind illustrates this very well:

To prove that he was stronger, the wind said to the sun one day, *"Do you see that man over there with all of those clothes on? I can blow them off of him and you will see that I am the greatest power." The sun just smiled and quietly accepted the challenge. So the wind blew and blew and blew some more, but the more he blew, the tighter the man pulled his clothes around him. When the wind could blow no more, it was the sun's turn. The sun shone on the man, warming him and slowly, little by little, the man began to shed his over clothes and then his clothes...*

While keeping my hands in accepting contact with Amy, I acknowledged her pain, fear and sadness with my words and in my hands that did not react or judge, by pushing, pulling, manipulating or breaking contact.

By the end of our time together, Amy's body was more relaxed. There had been a releasing of the tension that I had felt earlier in her abdomen, especially in her diaphragm area. Her breaths were deeper and slower and her face did not have the strained look on it that it had had when she first arrived. It's always amazing to me how much younger people look after a session!

Amy made an appointment for the following week and after we hugged she said, "I feel so much better, now. It's like I'm lighter," and she smiled. Her face glowed and she looked angelic.

Early the next morning I got a call at home. It was Amy, so excited she could hardly speak, "Linda! Linda!" she said, "The baby turned around!"

I was still half asleep, "What? It did?"

"Yes! During the night, I felt the baby turn around! I've made an appointment with the doctor, but I'm sure it did!"

"Oh Amy, I'm so happy!" I said, tears on my cheeks.

"I haven't even told my husband yet! I had to tell you first! I'll call you later after I see the doctor!"

Amy's doctor confirmed that the baby had indeed turned around. Five weeks later, she delivered a healthy baby boy using the Bradley Method of natural child birth, just as she had wanted.

CHAPTER 25

ON THE OUTSIDE LOOKING IN

After rupturing two lumbar disks, while working as a union carpenter, Kenny had to have them removed. It took him almost a year to get over the physical trauma of the surgery and some days, he still had terrible back pain, often radiating down the back of his right leg. On those days, he had to stay flat on his back in bed, with a pillow under his knees, to get any relief. Pain medication didn't help. Kenny was a big man, well over six feet tall and weighed about 230 pounds. Two years before his back injury, he had stopped drinking and had been a member of Alcoholics Anonymous ever since. The year before, his second wife had divorced him and taking their toddler son, moved in with another man.

Almost two years after Kenny's surgery, he still had enough bad days that his doctor had suggested more surgery, but he wasn't quite ready to go through surgery again and of course, the doctor had said, there are no guarantees. One morning, Kenny called in so much pain that he said he couldn't even stand up straight. He wanted a Touch session and we made an appointment for that afternoon, though he was concerned that he wouldn't be able to make it up the stairs to my office.

When he arrived, after painfully climbing the stairs, he stood at the door, face pale and body twisted forward and to the right. Once settled onto the table, using lots of pillows for support, he had some relief, but still had low back pain. I put my hand on the area of his lumbar spine, over his surgical scar, that he had indicated. He closed his eyes and sighed and we were silent for some time.

"When did the pain get bad again, this time?" I asked.

"Well, the pain is always there, you know, sort of nagging, but bearable. Early this morning, I was lying in bed reading and my cousin called. He told me that he was thinking about me and wondered how I was and we talked for awhile. Before he hung up, he mentioned that he was at his Mom's house and they were having a party for his birthday... Well, after I hung up the phone, I read a little bit more and then I started to get up and I couldn't! I was in such terrible pain, I couldn't move. So I waited a little while and then I tried to stand up, you know, rolling over, putting my knees on the floor and then trying to stand up, but when I did, I couldn't stand up straight. That's when I called you."

"Any thoughts or feelings about that phone call from your cousin?" I suggested.

Kenny opened his eyes for a moment, then closed them again. "Well, I did feel kind of irritated about the fact that they were having a party for him. Our birthdays are on the same day, you know, and my aunt doesn't live far from me and I wasn't even invited."

"Are you and your cousin close?"

"We used to be, but I don't see him much anymore. After my father died and my mother, brother and sister moved to Australia, well, I don't see my immediate family anymore. The last time was ten years ago when I flew over to see them."

"Do you miss them?"

"Naw. I don't need them. My Dad was a drunk, used to beat us all up, especially my Mom. He was in and out of the state psychiatric hospital to dry out. I can remember having to dress up with my brother and sister, then Mom would take us up to visit Dad. It was humiliating. Once, when I was thirteen, and Dad was beating Mom, I went after him with a kitchen knife and you know what? I was the one arrested, not him! I was big, even then. Well the cops and my aunt and even my

Mom told me that I should be ashamed of myself, trying to kill my father and all! After that, he never hit me again! When I was little, he used to hit me and the more I cried, the more he'd hit me until I'd be so scared, I'd pee my pants and then he'd make fun of me and call me a baby..."

"How terrible."

Kenny sighed, and was quiet for some time. I let my hands stay quiet and soft, one on the surgical scar area on his lower spine, another higher up on his back. They stayed in gentle contact with him, following his breaths and the subtle movements of his body under them. "My girlfriend and I ran away to San Francisco. I was sixteen, she was fifteen. I was a father just about the time I turned seventeen and pretty much a junkie, too. It was near the end of that year that I was arrested for dealing drugs and sent to prison. I remember being so scared and alone and one day, my Mom, brother and sister came to visit me. Mom said she felt glad that I was in prison because I couldn't get into any trouble there! They had come to say good-bye. Mom was born and raised in Australia and she was going home, Marty and Susan were going with her. Marty is four years older, so he was 21, Susan was about 16, I think. Anyway, that was the last I saw of them, until I went to visit fifteen years later. Haven't seen 'em since...."

"What about your aunt and cousins?"

"Well, I really haven't seen much of them since I was a kid. My grandparents had a farm and our family lived in a little cottage on the farm. My aunt, my father's sister, and her husband had a nice, big house not far from the farm. My father, being in and out of the psychiatric hospital, never had much of a job and though my mother worked, they always said we didn't have any money. Christmas, birthdays and other holidays were always a disappointment and of course, if Dad wasn't drunk, it was a good excuse to be drunk, so he always was by the end of the day. I can remember going over to my aunt's with my family and watching while my cousins opened all of their wonderful, expensive things: toy trucks, skates, bicycles, model planes and boats and, oh, the candy, too! They always had a huge Christmas tree with millions of lights. Then my aunt would hand us our presents. It was always socks! Damn socks! And she'd make this big production out of giving them to us. Of course we had already gotten the underwear and pajamas at home. Mom said we only had money for practical things. Well, then, after we'd open the socks, Mom would make this big fuss over them and say how wonderful they were and how much we needed them and then we'd have the kiss Aunt Flora and say thank you and all...."

"What was that like?"

His big back rose and fell and he was quiet. Then, I felt a trembling under my hands, and then his back heaved and he started to sob. Holding my hands more firmly in place, I let them stay in constant contact with his body, following it with each breath and sob. "Well...," he began again, "I was always the 'black sheep' of the family. I can remember when my Dad would be drunk and in a rage, my mother would always look at me and say, 'What did you do this time?' Aunt Flora would always lecture me about how hard my mother worked and that I should not give her a bad time and that I should be grateful to have a mother like her. But I was always on the outside, never a part of anything. Marty was the big brother, the man of the family and Susan was the baby, and a girl, but I was in the middle and it seemed no one noticed me."

"And you were left..."

"Yes, I was left out. And I was left out again, when my cousin called to say 'hi' and it was almost like he was rubbing my nose in it again, after all of these years. But I guess I've always felt like I was on the outside, looking in. Like I didn't belong. I've always been a loner...."

"Was that a choice?"

The hand over his scar felt some pulsing underneath it and his upper back became tight for a moment. Then he took a deep breath and again began to cry quietly.

"It's very painful, isn't it?"

He nodded.

After the session, he was able to get off of the table without much difficulty and said that his back was only a little "stiff" at that time.

The next day, I got a call from Kenny: the pain was completely gone and he'd just been outside mowing his lawn!

CHAPTER 26

A MEMBER OF THE HEMLOCK SOCIETY

Having been depressed for many years and on Prozac for the last year, Loretta, a seventy-three year old patient, decided that she didn't want to take the medication anymore. She commented, "I still was depressed, the Prozac just made it so I didn't care that I was."

On my first visit, Loretta sat, as she always did each time after that, in one of her long flannel Lanz night gowns that she wore backwards. The house had polished hardwood floors and was light and spacious, with an art deco flair. On the mantel was a white ceramic monkey, with long eyelashes and a bow in her hair holding a sign that said, "Screw the Golden Years!" Having had multiple surgeries over the past twenty years for everything from a brain tumor to open heart surgery, she had most recently been hospitalized for pneumonia and, being on IV antibiotics, had developed an intestinal infection that had resulted in chronic diarrhea and rectal bleeding. After doing an assessment and checking her vital signs, I asked about the medications she was taking.

"None of the medication was working," she began, "so three months ago, I decided to just stop taking all of my pills and for a while, I felt better. But Bill and I were in Florida for the past month and I'm exhausted and discouraged. I couldn't keep up with him. I felt like a burden...."

"Could you tell him that you're tired and need to rest?"

"Bill doesn't want to hear that I'm not feeling well. He thinks I should 'fight it' and will tell me how much better I look. I don't feel better. I'm so tired of 'fighting it' and now I have a sore throat and my doctor put me back on antibiotics, but she still thinks that there's something going on with my heart, again. She wants to do a stress test on Thursday, but I told her there was no point in doing it because I'm not having any more surgery! My children say to me, 'Mom, we're not worried because you've licked everything else and we know you can lick this, too.' And that's all they say. They don't want to know how I really feel. My husband's family is in Florida, and they're all older than we are and we're expected to care for them and to listen to them about all of their ailments, operations and pain..."

"What about your pain?" I asked.

"They never even ask. Even if people ask, 'How are you?' they don't really want to know. So when Bill asks, I just say, 'Fine,'" she said with a sigh.

"So how are you? And I really want to know."

"I have no strength anymore. I have to stop and catch my breath just to walk to the bathroom. I'm just so tired of the fight and I don't want to live anymore. I asked my doctor to help me to die."

"And what did she say?"

"She said that her mother is the same age as I am and that she just got back from a trip to China."

"What was that like for you?" I asked.

"Terrible!" Loretta said, face flushing momentarily, " It felt like she didn't even hear what I was saying!"

Loretta and I continued to talk for some time, mostly about her family and her physical symptoms and pain. When she told me that she was having pain in her back, over her left lung and felt a 'choking' feeling in her throat, I asked if I could touch her in those places. Making hands-on contact where the physical pain and tension are stored in the body, is often the gateway to healing. The gentle focus makes it possible to connect to those deeper levels of emotional and spiritual pain. After perhaps five minutes of Touch, quiet tears began to run down her pale cheeks, but she said nothing. Her breaths became deeper and slower and her body softened a little and with a sigh, she rested her head back against me as I stood behind her chair.

"That was very soothing, comforting and warm," she said when I was seated back next to her again. Then she looked me straight in the eyes and asked, "What do you think I should do?"

"Loretta, I know that you are in pain, but I don't know your pain. Pain is subjective, so only you know the extent of it. I believe you need to follow your heart. You know what you want and need to do."

She started crying, "All of the surgery that I have had, I never really wanted, but the doctors would say, 'If you won't think about yourself, at least think of your family and how terrible it would be for them if you were to die.' And do you know, the surgery only made me feel worse than before. It's been nothing but twenty years of pain and struggle."

She told me about her second child, who was born severely retarded and though she didn't want to, the doctors advised her to institutionalize the child and to have another child immediately to 'get over' that one. Her third child was asthmatic and was frequently hospitalized, several times near death, until she was finally institutionalized in an experimental program for two years. Her life story was full of losses and pain, the most significant of which was the loss of personal power.

"So," I asked, "now, in this moment, what really matters to you? What does Loretta want for Loretta?"

"I want to die. I'm worn out and I don't want to fight anymore. I'm a member of the Hemlock Society and though there hasn't been a meeting in town for over a year, I have the address of the minister involved in it. I think I'll write him."

"From what you've told me, your whole life has been a struggle, no wonder you're worn out."

Loretta smiled as some pink came back into her cheeks and her face relaxed. Her breathing was again deeper and slower as it had been when she was being touched. We laughed heartily when I suggested that the probable reason the local Hemlock Society hadn't had a meeting in over a year was that all of the members were dead. It was one of our ongoing jokes for the years that I knew Loretta.

There was a time, not long ago, that I would take a patient's expression of wanting to die personally. Where had I failed? Death is often viewed by doctors, nurses and others in modern medicine as the enemy. Today my view is totally different. It is not for me to judge the breadth and depth of a patient's pain. Relaying a story about another patient who has the same illness and has "fought it" or "overcome it," though seemingly well intentioned, is not appropriate at that particular time. (Though success stories about others in similar circumstances can and do give patients strength and hope.) The underlying message here is, if so and so did it, why don't you shut up and do it, too? It's a minimizing of someone else's pain, an invalidation of feelings. Instead of judging a patient's expression of pain and despair as self-pity, I can silently or verbally acknowledge my own feelings of discomfort, if I have any, as well as accepting that my patient is feeling like death is the only option at that moment.

I have seen Loretta many times over the last several years and though she has had a few more hospital admissions, she has had no more surgery. She has done more traveling, visiting her grandchildren and son in Texas and though she doesn't always have the strength that she'd like to have, she has chosen to live. There seems to have been a relaxing of the struggle for her, and each time I see her, she wants to be Touched. Often, recognizing and accepting that there is a struggle and having that struggle validated is all that is needed to begin to release it. Think of all of the energy we expend fighting to hold our perceived "negative" or shameful feelings inside. When last I spoke with her, she had planned a four month stay in Austin in a rented house that she describes as "gorgeous". It sure sounds like she wants to live.

CHAPTER 27

PAIN AND SPACE TRAVEL

While doing a weekend workshop on Touch in Livingston, Montana several years ago, I also had the opportunity to do some private sessions with many of the participants. One was a pretty woman in her early forties with deep, red hair.

As I always do before a working on someone, I spent some time talking with Rusty, getting a "feeling" for her and letting my intuition guide me. Because we had never met and I had no referral or medical record on her, I asked her about physical illnesses, disabilities, mental disorders, injuries and for any condition or problem, I wanted to be sure that she had been checked out by a medical doctor. Rusty reported nothing unusual in her history and her reason for wanting a session was that she felt she had a lot of tension, especially in her lower abdomen, which was painful at times. She said her doctor had run all kinds of tests which were all negative.

When I am doing Touch in the mainstream medical setting in conjunction with a skilled nursing visit, I modify the work to be fifteen to thirty minutes. For a full session, which runs about an hour to an hour and fifteen minutes, I ask the patient to undress if they are comfortable with that, because it's easier for me to feel changes with direct skin contact. (It's not necessary, though and in the modified sessions, the patient is either clothed or in nightclothes.) They are always draped for privacy, and lie on a massage table. Unless they are unable physically, or prefer not to, I ask them to begin the session face down on the table, the reason being that, for most people, this feels like a less vulnerable position than lying supine.

Rusty began by lying face down and the session was quiet and tender. Somewhere I had heard the expression "Drama does not heal trauma" and that is definitely true. Marion Rosen once said that "true feelings are quiet and deep." So for many of the sessions, there is often a silent connection and perhaps a single tear on the patient's cheek and then the session is over, and the patient feels much better, more relaxed, their pain has lessened or is gone and there may not have even been a conscious "ah ha!" but there is a release, a connection in a silent, deep place and it is good and right. I have found that people who tend to talk incessantly when they first come for a session, will become quiet when my hands are on them and for those patients of few words, well, they become very verbally expressive as soon as they are touched. With Touch, everyone gets what they need.

After perhaps twenty minutes, I asked Rusty to turn onto her back and, after draping her, I put my hands on the area of her abdomen that she had told me was tense and often painful. She lay quietly, eyes closed. Within a few moments, though, Rusty started breathing very rapidly and I could feel her pounding heart vibrating her body under my hands.

"What are you noticing?" I asked her.

"I'm in my room, the same room I had when I was a little girl and I'm in my bed and I'm really scared."

"How old are you?"

"I'm six," she whispered, "Shhh! It's Daddy!" then she was silent and held her breath. Another moment and Rusty started screaming not like a woman but like a little child.

"What's happening, Rusty?"

"It's Daddy! He's in my bed and it's dark! He's touching me down there and hurting me and he won't stop."

"Rusty, you can tell him to stop, right now!" I urged.

"No, I can't! He'll hit me! I can't make him stop!"

"You couldn't make him stop then because you were so little – you were only six, but the grown-up Rusty can tell him to stop."

"Stop! Stop! Get away!" she yelled and then she held her breath again.

"What happened, Rusty?" I asked, "Did he go away?"

"Yes," she whispered with a sigh, "he's gone..." and she started to sob, the tears emerging from behind her closed eyes. Rusty cried from way deep inside with such anguished wails that tears rolled down my cheeks.

"Did you know this about your father?" I asked.

"No... this was my first memory." She continued to cry for some time as I kept my hands in gentle contact with her abdomen that had softened considerably. Suddenly it tensed. She screamed: "Oooooo, nooo! They've come again, my God they've come for me again!"

"Who have come?" I asked, but she continued as if she didn't hear me.

"Now I'm in their spaceship and they have ugly green faces and they are drooling white, stinky stuff from their mouths and...," she screamed shrilly, eyes opened wide, "My God! Can't you see the aliens? What's the matter with you? Oh, nooooo, make them stop!"

"Who?" I asked trying not to show my concern. Did Rusty have a psychiatric history that she didn't tell me about? She was having a psychotic episode and I told myself that I should end the session. But another part of me argued that she had just had her first conscious memory of being sexually abused by her father and the pain had to be excruciating physically, emotionally, psychologically and spiritually. How would a six-year-old cope with something like that? Fantasies? Better aliens hurting her than her own father. Don't panic, I said to myself. No one ever gets more than they can handle.

"Aliens! The aliens! And they have impregnated me and ripped open my belly and are tearing at my flesh and they are eating my flesh and are killing my baby..."

I just had to be honest and direct and not go along with it, I thought. Then I said, "Okay, Rusty, Rusty? Do you hear me?"

"Yes!" she screamed, eyes fixed on the ceiling.

"Rusty, I'm having a hard time following you, here, would you please come back now? Come back into your body and tell me what you're feeling," I said firmly.

She screamed some more.

"Rusty! Listen to me! Come back into your body in this room right now, in this moment and tell me what you're feeling in your body. Are you in pain?"

"Yes! Yes, yes. It hurts, it hurts so much!"

"I hear you, Rusty. You are in terrible pain right now," I said softly, "It's painful to know that your father hurt you...."

"Yes," she said more in a normal tone, closing her eyes as she began to cry again.

"Rusty," I said softly, after some time, "What do you need from me?"

"I need to be held."

So I wrapped her upper body in my arms and held her close, rocking her like a little child, and she sobbed.

After the session, Rusty was more relaxed. She said that her abdomen felt pain-free and relaxed, her face looked ten years younger. Through the center that sponsored the workshop, Rusty was referred to a therapist who specialized in helping people with incest issues. When I recently spoke with her therapist, she told me that Rusty had made great progress and the "alien" incident has never reoccurred.

Chapter 28

The Orient Express

The housekeeper escorted me into the bedroom where Charles, ill with throat cancer, smiled at me from the bed. He was fully dressed, wore wire rims and had been reading before I had walked in and introduced myself. A slender man in his late sixties, he nodded, then with a raspy voice said:

"Mary's in the bathroom," as he pointed to the door in the far corner of the room, "Go on in, she's expecting you." It amazed me then and still does, that though I was a total stranger, because I was the nurse, I had been whisked right into their bedroom, then directed to the bathroom. Some may not consider this an honor, but I do, though it is not so much physical location but rather what being there represents. Only my closest friend or significant other is invited into the privacy of my bedroom or bath, so this feels to me like I am extended an almost immediate trust.

Another of the many things that I love about being a visiting nurse is that I don't wear a uniform. I have my own style of dressing and love to wear fun and interesting clothes. Frequenting consignment and vintage clothing shops, I avoid malls because of the crowds and because to me, all of the clothes look the same. The two owners of one of my favorite consignment shops always keep me informed when "new" clothes come in that they know I'll like!

That day, as I knocked softly on Mary's bathroom door, I was wearing a flowing, silk batik jacket in lavenders, purples, black and rusts with a primitive lion crouched on the back. Mary opened the door. She was very thin and pale and, having just been discharged from the hospital that morning, still wore a white and blue hospital gown that tied in the back. She was carrying a small tank of oxygen whose attached transparent green tubing looped in her hand then under the front of her gown. She was noticeably short of breath, the muscles in her neck and shoulders were working hard, but before I could introduce myself, her eyes opened wide:

"OOOOoooooo!" she exclaimed, "What a beautiful jacket!"

"Thank you."

"Turn around! Turn around and let me see you!" she commanded.

I spun around.

"Walk across the room! Ooooo, Charles, did you see this jacket?"

"Very nice," Charles commented, looking up from his book.

"Charles," Mary said, "Where's the camera? I want to get a picture of...what was your name?"

"Linda."

"...Linda in her jacket!"

I modeled my jacket for Mary and she snapped a few photographs. "Turn around now," she said, "and look back over your shoulder at me so I can get a picture of you and the lion on the back!"

After that I said, "Now it's your turn to try on the jacket and be photographed!"

"Oh, no, no, no, no, no!" Mary said as she continued to gasp for breath between words, "I look terrible!"

"You look like you just got sprung from the hospital! Come on," I encouraged, "Try it on." I took the jacket off and held it up for her to put on. She hesitated momentarily then plunged her arms into the sleeves before walking back and forth like a model on a runway. I photographed her, giggling at the "look" that was, I told her, the rage in Paris this season: flowing, silk batik jackets over your basic hospital gown. A fashion statement in contradiction. In fashion as in life.

The fashion show over, I finally got down to doing my "nurse stuff" and checked Mary's lungs, blood pressure and did a physical assessment. Because of her COPD (chronic obstructive pulmonary disease) she needed to wear oxygen at all times. During this last stay in the hospital, she had had her oxygen tubing inserted in her abdomen, just under the skin, and threaded directly into her trachea so that she didn't have to wear a nasal cannula.

"I did it for several reasons," she said, "first because my little granddaughter seems to be afraid of me when I wear it. She always says, 'Grandma, why do you have that green thing on your face?' Secondly, my nose and sinuses were always so dried out and thirdly, the oxygen is more concentrated this way. I think I'm going to like it: now I can put my portable tank in a little tote bag and you'll hardly be able to tell I'm using oxygen."

After examining Charles, I hugged them both goodbye and promised another visit soon. I remember feeling so grateful, as I drove to my next patient's house, that not only did I feel that I was making a difference in my patients' lives, I was having so much fun, too! I had not done Touch on Mary or Charles that day, though they both said they wanted to try it, but we had touched in other ways. It was several weeks later when I saw them again. Charles had just had chemotherapy and was resting, so after checking him over and spending some time with him, Mary and I sat at the kitchen table over cups of herbal tea.

"So I said to Charles, 'Charles! Are we both going to sit around her feeling sick and sorry for ourselves?' And I answered, 'Not me, how about you?' and he said that he didn't want to either and that he wanted to live the life he had left, doing what he always wanted to do, so I called my travel agent, and told her that I wanted her to book us our dream vacation: a trip on the Orient Express!"

"Wow! Good for you! When do you want to go?"

"Next month. We don't have time to waste," Mary said, getting tears in her eyes, then taking a sip of tea before continuing: "Well, my friends told me that I was crazy and that the Orient Express is booked years in advance. But I called my travel agent anyway and told her that we needed to go next month, and you know, she called me back the same day: there had just been a cancellation! So we're going!"

"Great! What about help for you and Charles?" I asked.

"Not to worry, we've each got a nurse coming with us, and they're arranging for my oxygen, too."

"I really admire you both for your courage and faith. Life is so precious and time is meant to be treasured...what a wonderful example you are... It feels right, doesn't it?"

Mary nodded before we hugged.

Three months later, when visiting, I happened to be wearing my Silk Batik Lion Jacket. "I'm so glad you wore that jacket!" Mary smiled.

"As I was the first time we met."

"That's right."

"But, though you can't really see it," I said, holding the back of the loose left sleeve up, "I caught this on a doorknob and it tore."

"Give it to me, I'll fix it," she said, examining the damaged sleeve, "I used to do a lot of fine needlework."

"Really?" I asked, "You'll fix that for me?"

"Sure, leave it here and it'll be done by the time I see you again."

I took off the jacket and handed it to her, "Why don't you wear it to your family reunion?" I offered.

"Oh no! I couldn't do that, I'd feel terrible if something happened to it!"

"You're more than welcome to wear it, in fact, I'd love for you to wear it."

"Well," she smiled, "maybe I will...."

Mary and I sat at the kitchen table, envelopes of photographs piled high:

"Here we are in Venice, and look here: here's Charles in the back of the gondola, look how happy he is!"

"He looks healthy, too," I added, "his color is great and he looks like he had put on a little weight here, doesn't he?"

"Yes," she smiled, "I hadn't seen him eat with such gusto in over a year. It was wonderful...oh, look, this is my favorite one," Mary whispered, tears in her eyes, as she handed me a photograph of them elegantly dressed, standing on the platform in front of the grand old Orient Express. Charles wore a finely tailored tweed suit and Mary was in a classic sweeping ankle length dress with a matching hat cocked to one side. She was carrying her matching tote bag, oxygen tank concealed. A tear rolled down my cheek. I looked up at Mary, who was wiping her face before taking a deep breath. Suddenly she said, "Oh!" getting up from her chair, "Come with me! I have to show you something!" I followed her into the dining room and there, on the sideboard, was a miniature replica of the Orient Express. It was finely crafted down to the last detail and even had little lamps in some of the windows. "This was the car we were in," she said quietly, pointing to a deep green and cream colored car. "This is Charles' train," she said, her voice breaking.

"You had a lovely time, didn't you?"

"It was the dream of a lifetime...He had two weeks of remission and feeling good so we could share one last, special time together...Charles' last gift to me: these wonderful memories. It was even better than our honeymoon, fifty-two years ago."

That day, and since then, Mary has asked me to Touch her and has shared more of herself with me as I have with her. During those times, the tension in her neck, shoulders and chest lessens and her breathing becomes slower and easier. She tells me how much she loves being touched and that when we are together, her feelings well up inside of her, though most other times she is not aware of them. Often she has said that she wishes she could give me what I have given her and I tell her she has already given me so much:

Mary's enthusiasm and joie de vie always affirms that life is precious, a gift to be treasured. I continually hold that grand picture in my heart and mind's eye of Mary and Charles standing regally on the platform in front of 'Charles' train.' At the formal gala they attended one night on the Orient Express: I see them arriving arm in arm, he crisp and proud in his tuxedo, she elegant and trim in her cream-colored satin gown. I imagine that holding their chilled, golden glasses together as they drank a toast "To Life!"

Chapter 29

I Been There

Perhaps it was because I spent my childhood and teen years living in a "war zone" with a pistol-wielding, alcoholic father who had also been traumatized by war. Maybe it was that I grew up in the sixties and had some friends that fought in the Vietnam War. The reasons didn't really matter – somehow I felt connected to Peter, a Vietnam Vet, even before our first meeting.

He had kept a diary, written from the heart and in the lingo of that time, of his experiences and the wisdom that allowed him to survive the war. Peter had recorded something one of his friends had said to him one day about being in Vietnam: "I remember a teacher I had in high school telling us that we didn't have to travel to Africa to know its geography. I don't believe it. If you never had to crawl through a rice paddy that smelled like shit, with leeches sucking your skin, in 110 degree heat, with a bad case of the craps, and your feet itching and your toes rotting away in your wet boots which you've had on for a month – and while you're feeling like this, you've got an unknown number of Vietnamese Soldiers who are tryin to give you a very bad headache with a bullet in your forehead, then you haven't been there. I mean, get real! You can think you know what something feels like, but if you haven't been there and had my experience, you're really not going to feel what I felt, and I'm not going to know how you felt either. It's really not important if we haven't had a particular experience. What is important is that we really listen to each other so we can share our experiences..."

We had talked on the phone several times before I finally met the tall, slender soft-spoken man with wire rim glasses. I remember being completely surprised by his gentleness, because the diary he had written about his experiences in Vietnam (which I had read before our meeting), filled with the hard language that helped him to survive, seemed to have been written by a man that I had imagined would have been big and tough in appearance.

After the war, Peter slept in the hold of an anchovy boat, made five dollars a day selling the day's catch, and through smoking pot and drinking alcohol was, as he described it "out there" most of the time. One day, he met a follower of Maharishi who convinced him that he would find himself and happiness if he became a follower. Giving up drugs and learning meditation, Peter, who was creative and intelligent quickly moved up in the ranks and became closely and deeply involved with the Maharishi. But, though he had gotten much from being a follower, he was increasingly aware of his deep anguish which, in a group where "bliss" was the goal, made him feel like he had failed.

Leaving the flock and using his talents, Peter became very successful in the advertising business, traveled extensively and lived on a nice expense account. Constantly wined and dined, cocktails at lunch and dinner and in between became the norm and soon Peter, married and with three children, had become an alcoholic.

He started going to a twelve-step program for alcoholics and, after being sober for several years, Peter joined a Vietnam Vets group that was run by a psychotherapist, where he began to get in touch with some of his feelings. He found much support and validation from those in the group who had "been there." Up until that time, he never spoke about his experiences in Vietnam and didn't want to admit that he was a vet. Though he had stopped drinking, and was going to the group, he was experiencing uncontrollable outbursts of rage, bouts of depression and unhappiness in his marriage. Having had back pain and a feeling of being "wound up tight" for years, one of his friends suggested that he have some kind of body-centered work. This was about the time that he called for an appointment.

Though he had gotten much help from the therapist and support from the men in his group, he said that for some time he felt that he just couldn't go any deeper.

"One time," he said, "I got in touch with this emotional stuff, very gory and disturbing from a time in Vietnam. And when I started to unleash those feelings, the therapist completely shut me off. Like she didn't want to deal with it!"

During his Touch sessions, Peter experienced feelings of rage, grief terror, tenderness and love. Very often, he told me, that he felt that when my hands were on him, we were connected and that sometimes it even felt like my hands were actually inside of him. Something very profound can happen when two people touch. It is not just a physical connection but a joining of the minds and spirits. Many times, I am aware that there is something with us in the room, a higher intelligence that guides us both. It is at those times that I experience a deep "knowing" that affirms me and the person I am with. It's a feeling of being completely and utterly safe and connected to myself and that person and cradled, rocked and bathed in pure love.

One day, after feeling and expressing profound sadness, Peter said that he felt like a little boy. "I feel silly asking," he began, "but I need to be held. Will you hold me?"

I wrapped my arms around his upper body, as he lay face up on the table, and cradled him like a small child in my arms as he sobbed.

When I hold and Touch my patients, I am often moved to tears, feeling a sensation deep in my chest where my heart is. I recognize it as the same feeling I have toward my own daughter, a feeling so profound that the word love doesn't seem enough to describe it. Tender as well as fierce, I feel like a lioness protecting her cub. It's an unshakable "knowing" that this person before me is already complete and whole. The protectiveness I feel is undoubtedly because in that moment they are so open, vulnerable and completely trusting.

When someone is in pain, it touches my pain. When someone is in despair, it touches those places in all of us. Though many of us are often unaware of our pain, it still exists. Connecting in pain often allows us the openness and vulnerability needed to experience pure Love, which is our true nature. I heard once that everything we do is Love seeking to know itself.

For Peter and many others, life is war and every day feels like a fight to stay "alive". It seems that they are struggling against addictions, jobs, relationships and just getting through the day. The battle really lies within. The tension, pain and energy it takes to keep perceived "unacceptable" and even "dangerous" feelings out of sight and out of mind is tremendous. Too often, people don't separate feelings from behaviors. There are no unacceptable or dangerous feelings only unacceptable and dangerous behavior. Awareness of these feelings and our power to choose our action is the first step toward healing.

Peter recently said, "There's something about being touched that makes me feel safe to kind of let it out...maybe it's because your hands are on me, kind of like a mother's touch... After a session I feel more "open," more aware of my feelings, closer to myself and more relaxed. It's like I'm daring to feel and I'm open to life!"

Chapter 30

So Brief a Verse

Norton had multiple sclerosis and at the time I started doing home visits to his apartment, he had become a quadriplegic so was only able to move from his neck up. He was fifty-two with a wonderful sense of humor and resonant voice with which he commanded his domain:

"Abraham!" he said with great authority to his Voice Butler on the table next to his bed.

"Yes, Master?" it responded appropriately.

"Equator!"

"Yes, Master?"

"Turn off!"

"Yes, Master!" and immediately the space heater above Norton's bed shut off.

"Wow!" I said, having never seen a Voice Butler before, "That's great. I love that he called you master and he obeyed."

"The way it should be," grinned Norton, "and he answers the phone for me and can make a call out if I need him to."

Over the next eight months, I saw Norton three to four times a week. He had nurse's aides that bathed, fed and kept him company for four hours in the morning and four hours in the evening. The rest of the time he was alone and physically helpless in his bed. He had a "lifeline" pinned to his pillow, so if he needed emergency help, he could turn his head and use his cheek to push the button that would immediately call 9-1-1 for him.

Besides doing dressing changes on his bedsore that seemed like it would never heal, the nurses would come in twice a day to give him anticoagulant injections. I never liked giving injections, though I'd rather give them than get them, but I especially dislike giving Heparin because it's given into the abdomen. Though patients tell me that it doesn't hurt any more in their bellies than anywhere else, it still makes me cringe when I give them.

One morning as I gave Norton his Heparin injection, I said, "OOooo, poor baby."

He smiled, "I'm not sure why, but I liked it when you said, 'poor baby.'"

Norton had been a photographer and I did free-lance photography part time. He was also a great reader and lover of poetry as well as a poet, as was I. We shared our photographs and poetry with one another.

As time went on, he began to have more and more pain in his body. Though he understood that we had to turn him and care for him and would never ask us to stop, he would scream every time we turned him or touched him. His screams were loud and anguished, "Please hurry, please hurry!" he would beg, crying with pain. And the aide and I would work as fast as we could to clean him and finish his care.

Norton's voice became so soft and broken and often, Abraham did not even respond. Frequently he seemed like he wasn't even in his room, let alone in his body. His eyes didn't have their same mischievous twinkle and his breaths were rapid and shallow because of the pain, though he was being medicated frequently.

One morning, Norton said in a whisper, "Don't tell anyone that I'm saying this to you because they'll get upset and send in a psychiatrist and I don't need one. What I need is to die. If I could, I'd commit suicide."

"It sounds like you've had enough."

"I have," came his coarse whisper.

I felt tears on my cheeks. "Norton, I hear you and when you are ready, you will leave."

He looked surprised, even hopeful for a moment, "How?"

"You will, you just will, and if it didn't hurt you for me to touch you, I'd rock you like a baby."

He smiled.

"So just imagine that you are being rocked in my arms...."

He smiled again and closed his eyes.

"You are safe and loved and it's a beautiful day, warm and soft and you can feel the sunlight on your face. And imagine a place that you want to be, a special place that is safe and comfortable..." and then I sang him a lullaby.

Not more than four days later, Norton was taken to the hospital where he died.

Plans had been made to move him to a convalescent home, it was never to be. Norton was ready and when someone is ready, they will leave. Death, for him, was a healing. And it was up to those of us remaining here who loved him to grieve his loss.

I wish there had been a course when I was in nursing school called something like, "Death 101" on how to be with a dying patient. But perhaps it couldn't be taught, at least not in a classroom. My teachers have been my patients and it has taken many years. As a nurse, I feel that I had to come to some sort of terms with my own mortality before I could really be present for my patients. I love the idea of Hospice where the goal is to support patients and their families lovingly as they go through death and loss. Years ago, I used to take the death of a patient as a personal affront, almost as my failure as a nurse and would spend as little time as possible with a dying patient. It was too scary for me, a reminder of the loss of my mother, a reminder of my own mortality.

My patients have taught me that dying is easier, yes even welcome when a person has lived life to the fullest. Every moment is precious and it's important to cherish each day and follow our dreams.

Now, I consider it an honor to be present in someone's last days and hours. Very simply, it comes down to doing all that we humanly can and then letting go of the outcome. Norton and the rest of my patients have been loving teachers and I am grateful to have known them all.

Chapter 31

Diane's Blue Sky

Diane's dark hair and smooth, rosy complexion set her physically apart from most of the elderly patients, but what really attracted me to her was her free spirit and hearty laugh. In a wheelchair since the age of thirty-one, Diane came to live at Heritage Heights from an independent living facility because she needed total care. Now in her mid forties, she could not walk, was incontinent and because she had no small motor coordination, could not feed herself. She was a large woman and so was very difficult to move out of bed into her wheelchair.

Diane recalled the moment vividly in 1979 when her doctor told her that she had multiple sclerosis: "I remember looking out of the window of his office and wishing that I could fly away."

Those times that I did Touch on Diane, she said she didn't notice a difference afterwards. I had only been doing Touch for perhaps a year on my own, then, and I guess I thought that either I hadn't done something the "right" way or that maybe it wasn't right for Diane. Looking back, though, I have to say that it *did* make a difference in her life and in mine. Maybe we both expected that the Touch would make a change in the course of her illness, would give her more strength, more coordination. Maybe we were hoping for a physical change to occur. I had thought then, that Touch didn't work for her. Well, I have been wrong and if it were any bigger or more obvious it would have bit me. Arne, one of my teachers once said that whenever we touch someone, there is a change. When Diane and I met, and she allowed me to Touch her with my hands, our hearts also touched, and because of that, two years later, a dream came true...

This day had been two years in coming, so when the alarm rang in the blackness of 4:30 am, I was up and on my way in no time. Arriving at Heritage Heights, Diane had already been dressed and transferred to her wheelchair by the hydraulic Hoyer lift and was beaming when I entered the small room that she shared with two women almost twice her age.

"It's finally here!" I grinned, "Did you ever think that this day would come?"

"Oh yes, yes, I knew it would come sooner or later, and if it had happened last year, we wouldn't have today to look forward to." Diane said with her usual optimism and amazing patience.

Diane is an adventurer but is limited to where the Sweethart buses with the wheelchair lifts will take her. Often Diane and I will cruise the mall and have lunch. She has to be fed and drinks with a straw – even beer. Our standard joke is, when Diane has a beer, we have to tighten up the seat belt on her wheelchair.

When I left my job as nursing supervisor, Diane gave me a surprise "retirement" party. She had arranged to have a cake and fresh strawberries with chocolate and whipped cream to dip them in. I don't know how it started, though I'm sure Diane must have encouraged it, but there was a food fight between myself and one of the evening nurses with whipped cream in her ear and soda in my hair. Diane got caught in the crossfire of whipped cream and she laughed so much that tears streamed down her face behind her glasses. She waved her hands and begged, "Stop! Stop!" With Diane it's always easy to laugh.

So here it was, two years later. The idea for this adventure began one night when Diane told me that she wanted to try bungee jumping.

"Bungee jumping? You are crazy!"

"Yes, yes!" she laughed.

"Well, I always knew you were."

"That's why we get along so well. Birds of a feather..."

"Hard to believe we're two women in our forties, isn't it?"

Because of my veto, bungee jumping was out, but we agreed on "alternate plan B." We planned and schemed and all of the nurses and other staff at Heritage Heights said that we were crazy (which we had already decided) and that it would never happen because Diane was a big woman and in a wheelchair, no less. They said that there was no way it could be done.

Coordinating the plan and the logistics was not easy, but Diane has been a good teacher: though she is earthbound and completely dependent on others for her physical care, her spirit literally soars. She had every confidence that her dream would come true, and so today, it would.

After putting on her base make-up, blush and lipstick and fixing her hair, I found her coat in the closet and pulled it on over her arms. My friend, Jonathan, arrived to help and to take video and photographs.

It was 5:45 am on that cool September morning, still dark, but Bill, from the bus company, was waiting for us outside. Diane was lifted, wheelchair and all, into the bus with its hydraulic lift and, after Bill secured her in place, we were on our way to meet Paul and Valerie Moorlock at a nearby shopping center.

Paul sent up a little black balloon into the grayness of the predawn sky, consulted with Valerie and then giving a thumbs up, nodded to us: "We're going to Roxbury, so you follow us!"

Some of the earlier morning fog had disappeared, but there were still thick pockets along the twisting country roads. It seemed like we would never get there. Diane, Bill and I kept trying to guess where we'd be stopping every time we'd see an open field. Though lots of people had been enthusiastic about the trip and wanted to be a part of it, their excitement waned when they realized they'd have to meet us at six in the morning. So we were a small band of adventurers: the Moorlocks in their van, followed by Diane, Bill and I in the Sweethart bus with Jonathan in his red Toyota pickup bringing up the rear. I worried a little about having only three men to lift Diane, but when I saw her face glowing in the dark bus, I knew it would work out.

Our little caravan stopped in a field behind the town hall in Roxbury, where Paul and Valerie went to work immediately. Pulling unending yards of red,white and blue nylon out of a bag and laying it straight out on the ground until it extended about a hundred feet, they turned on a big generator-powered fan that began to lift the nylon up and fill the inside with air. Bill had brought Diane out onto the lift platform on the side of the bus so she could watch the preparations, before he jumped right in to helping Paul and Valerie. He spread the nylon and held it open so the air could fill it more easily, like a pro, though he told me this was his first time.

The air billowed inside the nylon, making it look like a red, white and blue beached whale. At this point, Paul lit up the big gas flame on the top of the basket and laying it sideways at the opening, filled the foundering "whale" with hot air until it floated weightlessly upright.

The next step was getting Diane into the basket. Miraculously, during the process of setting up, Dave, a friend of the Moorlocks, had seen the preparations in passing on his way to work and stopped to join us. So that now we had four men to lift Diane into the basket! Positioning the basket right next to the lift of the bus, Diane was lifted from her wheelchair to the edge of the basket, then lowered onto and belted into a chair inside, her head just above the rim so that she could see out.

I had been a little nervous about the flight, but suddenly I felt afraid. Diane was grinning ear to ear, her eyes sparkled like a child's at Christmas and the next thing I knew, we were off of the ground and instantly my fear was gone. It didn't even feel like we lifted off, it was more like we floated up. As our captain, Paul, pulled the lever of the flame and filled the hot air balloon with more and more hot air, we drifted upwards and the only sensation that I had that we were even moving up was that the Sweethart bus, the van and the red pickup were getting smaller and smaller. Diane and I waved to our ground crew.

After two years of planning and canceled flights due to risky weather, we were finally airborne! There was barely a breeze, as I thought there would be. It was then that I realized, we were the breeze.

The best indication of movement up in the balloon was by watching its shadow move across the landscape. The view to the west was early fall colors, mixed with deep green that was separated by pockets of moving fog which looked exactly like whipped cream. We floated over sleepy farms, fields and a misty pond so quietly that not even the grazing horses twitched an ear. We rose higher and higher. To the east, the sun was just up, white beams reaching horizontally over waves and shadows of fog that, though we were inland, looked like the rugged New England coastline.

Losing altitude, we watched as the treetops drew nearer. What if we got caught in the trees, I wondered. Diane was ecstatic and throwing her head back, laughed out loud. Our basket perched momentarily on the treetops and Paul said calmly, "We're just like the birds."

Captain Paul brought our hot air balloon, the Fair Play, softly down next to a paved cul-de-sac in an undeveloped subdivision.

Paul had kept in constant radio contact with Valerie, who was following us in the van. Jonathan and Dave had gone off to their jobs and so Bill would be following her in the bus. Once Valerie had lost visual contact with us, it took her some time to find us, and so we waited. My thoughts turned to concern about getting Diane out of the balloon's basket. Four men had some difficulty getting her in and that was with gravity on their side. Now we had to get her out with two fewer men. Momentarily, I pictured us having to call the fire department, then decided not to worry because Diane's first comment when we were on the ground was: "That was so soft and fluffy."

The morning was clear, cool and beautiful. The Fair Play towered next to the huge oak and maple trees that surrounded us. Paul and Valerie talked back and forth on the radio until, coming up the road from behind the trees, I saw their van. Following was Bill in the the red, white and blue bus. As Diane has always said, "People are always talking about how bad the world is...they say that people are not nice, but I've always found the opposite to be true. The world is a wonderful place, filled with good people." Indeed, though I had my doubts at times, Diane never lost her faith for one moment. Not only did Valerie and Paul Moorlock agree to take Diane up in their balloon, they did so at no charge. The Sweethart Bus Company arranged to have Bill Council pick Diane up in the wee hours of the morning for her special trip, again at no cost. And somewhere, in the back of my mind, where I thought it was through my efforts that this trip had come about, in the next instant, that thought evaporated like the morning fog: following the bus was Jonathan's red pickup and then, lo and behold, someone else in a silver-gray sedan! Bud, another friend of the Moorlocks, had seen their balloon and followed the caravan!

Though they had trouble getting Diane out of the basket on the first try, it was Bill who suggested that they lift Diane, chair and all, up onto the rim. That worked very well and they were able to then transfer her from there to the waiting wheelchair on the raised lift platform of the bus.

Diane's courage and faith have been an inspiration to me. She's an example of how nothing can contain the human spirit if we choose to let it soar. From the moment that Diane decided that she would fly in a hot air balloon, her faith never wavered. Before our flight, it seemed to me that we had been "lucky" in finding giving people with good hearts, willing to help make Diane's dream come true. But that was not what really happened. Luck had nothing to do with it, nor did my individual efforts. It was beyond belief, beyond faith: it was a "knowing." Diane knows. She knows that the world is beautiful and that people are good and because that's what she expects, it is so. She knew that she would float all "soft and fluffy" and that she would be cared for and safe and so she was. It seems to me, as I look back over the years that I've known Diane, that she expects to laugh and have fun and meet good people and she does. She talks to everyone and everyone responds to her with the love that she radiates.

"I've been on some good trips in my life," Diane has said again and again since our adventure, "but that was the best. Definitely, that was the best."

On the wall near her bed in the room that she shares with two women nearly twice her age hangs a framed certificate. It's printed on paper that looks like a blue, fluffy sky and confirms that Diane Leonard did indeed ascend into the sky in a hot air balloon on September 21, 1994. It includes the following verse:

> *The winds have welcomed you with softness. The sun has blessed you with his warm hands. You have flown so high and so well that God has joined you in your laughter and set you gently back into the loving arms of Mother Earth. May your skies always be blue, your winds gentle and your landings soft.*

Chapter 32

What I Learned Along the Way

It has occurred to me many times while writing this book, that what I have learned along the way does not only apply to my professional life. There has been a total change in my view of myself, others and the world that has affected my personal life as well. What is exciting to me is that Touch and my new way of being a nurse which had, at first, uncovered, defined and enhanced my relationship with myself and then my patients, has now enriched all of my relationships. I am, for the most part, happily human and accepting of my limitations and imperfections. But here, again, since I'm human and can't be perfect at anything all of the time, I'm not perfect at being human, either. It's just now, when I sometimes catch myself not wanting to admit that I could possibly be imperfect at imperfection, well, it's kind of like a black hole with a sense of humor, isn't it?

Recently one of my students of Touch became angry when she perceived that I had "rescued" another student from her painful feelings. Earlier in the day, I had pointed out that she had wanted to do the same and "fix" someone else's pain. She was indignant because she believed that I had been inconsistent. I said nothing at the time that she confronted me because I felt embarrassed and didn't quite know what to say. After all, I was the teacher, wasn't I supposed to be perfect? Had I been inconsistent? Probably. I could have danced around the issue, made some excuses or explained how the circumstances were completely different or something like that, but that was not the point. What could I learn from this? What could we both learn? Well the lesson for me was, yes, Linda, you are inconsistent at times because you're human. The lesson for my student (she told me later) was that inconsistency from "Authority Figures" enraged her. Those awarenessess have greatly helped us both: awareness first, acceptance, then empowerment.

As a nurse, I see my job as one of empowering my patients. Being empowered means having self-trust and a willingness to accept one's present situation. From this place, patients can make decisions about the kinds of treatments and practitioners that are right for them. It's a letting go of ego and the delusion that we have control over others. I empower them, the same way I empower myself: by really listening to what they are saying verbally and non-verbally; by really seeing them, looking at them, their surroundings, the life they have chosen; by Touching them and by honoring and affirming their inner wisdom and ability to make the right choices.

In reality, the wonders of mainstream medicine do not heal but rather facilitate healing. It is the wisdom of the body, mind and spirit that heals, it is an acceptance of what is and faith in something greater than oneself. In the letting go of delusions that we can control the world, comes an acceptance of personal responsibility and therein lies profound healing. It is in that moment when we accept our human limitations that we become completely open to the limitlessness of Love. Touch is merely a vehicle that taps into each person's innate wisdom – first for awareness, then acceptance and then empowerment to know where we are and where we choose to go.

With map in hand, I have to know where I am before I can set off on my journey. If I am unable to admit that I am lost, I would never even get out the map, let alone ask someone for directions! How would I know which direction I need to travel, if I don't know where I am to begin with? In that moment when I pinpoint my location, I am empowered, knowing that I will be moving in the right direction. What I can offer my patients and others is an honest view of their reality by giving them feedback as to what I see, hear, feel and sense intuitively.

Personal power

George was in the last stages of a terminal illness. Though he sensed somewhere deep inside of him that he was dying, he had not consciously addressed this. His moods would swing from anger to despondency. Having refused visits from lifelong friends and having been nasty to his immediate family, he consequently had been spending a lot of time alone, brooding in his room. What I sensed was that he was afraid and grieving, and justifiably so. After doing my "nurse stuff" (a great way to get in the door of a room where no one is welcomed) I asked George how he was feeling.

"You're the nurse, you tell me!" he snapped.

"You sound angry." I observed, quietly.

"Of course I'm angry, wouldn't you be?"

"I'm sure I would be. You have a right to your feelings. What makes you the most angry?"

"Oh, I don't know," he said, his voice breaking as he turned his face away.

"That you're dying?"

Momentarily startled, he looked back up at me, then his eyes filled with tears and he nodded slowly. We were quiet for some time then George said, "What really breaks my heart is that I have a young grandson, eight years old. He's wonderful but I haven't wanted to see him lately. I feel so cheated that I won't be able to see him grow up...that I will be missing all of that...I feel helpless. I'm afraid I'll fall apart if he comes to see me..." he choked.

"You might want to write him a letter or do a video for him telling him how much you love him and that you're going to miss him. It would be something he could always keep. You could pick out something of yours that is very special to leave to him..."

George's face lit up and I sensed new energy. "Yes!" he said, smiling, "yes and I know just the thing! Actually there are several special things that I could leave to him and my oldest son has a video camera..."

The renewed energy in George came from his feeling of empowerment. He had recognized and accepted his present reality and, with that conscious knowledge, had made the choice to take back his personal power so he could positively effect what remained of his life.
My experience has demonstrated time and time again that we all are surprised by and greatly appreciate honesty, if offered without criticism or judgement. From self-awareness begins the evolution to self-acceptance, personal responsibility and then empowerment, where we can all make the choices that are right for us.

Touching, connecting, healing

My vision is that eventually Touch and all that accompanies it will become a normal, natural and integral part of mainstream medicine. When we touch someone, we have made a difference. Though I prefer to physically touch and be touched, we can "touch" or "connect" with someone on a very deep level in many ways: by looking at a person and really seeing him, listening to that person and really hearing her, by respecting our patients and others enough to be a gentle witness to their uniqueness rather than rushing in (as a lot of us in the helping professions do) to offer advice or to "fix it". That is not to say that I don't do my job as a registered nurse – I do all of the appropriate "nurse stuff" (first, if needed) then offer Touch as part of our time together. As time and circumstances allow, "touch" may be the taking of a hand, a knowing smile and really seeing and hearing a patient. It may also be fifteen minutes of placing hands on a painful or stressed area of the body (and it may include all of the above). We all need to be looked at, listened to and touched: this is a place of profound healing.

Healing involves more than just the absence of illness. Healing is a sense of peace and well-being of body, mind and spirit and you can't have one without the other two. When my mother was ill, what I saw was separation, indeed a polarization of the mainstream medical (physical) camp and the religious (spiritual) camp. This demand for "loyalty" left her confused and disjointed at a time when synthesis and peace of mind would have given her a better chance for recovery. Had that "recovery" even been acceptance and a gentle passing, that would have been a gift.

Mom used to say that we should live each day both as if it were our last and as if we were going to live forever. Living each day as if it were my last would mean that I'd have no time for anything that didn't really matter to me and that each moment would be precious. Living each day as if I were going to live forever would slow me down. It would help me get beyond the "there's not enough time to do it all and be it all" frenzy. Simple, but not easy.

We live in a time when we all can enjoy the benefits of scientific progress, but there is a time and a place for high-tech medicine: technology can never be a substitute for basic human needs. At the core of every human being is the need to love and be loved and Love is the very essence of who we are. The success of new technology depends completely on it being administered with humanity, caring and love.

Today I am proud to say I'm an R.N. I am privileged to an almost immediate trust and am escorted into bedrooms and bathrooms and privy to many intimate details of my patients' lives. Now, as a nurse, I can "touch" others in ways that I never could before, and I know that my presence has made a difference in their lives. What's more, to my delight, my patients bring much richness, fun, and joy into my life as well. When I am with a patient, my hands on her painful shoulders, and I feel the steel hardness begin to tremble, then pulsate with new feelings, and tears spill quietly down her cheeks as she takes in a deep breath, I share her pain and her joy and am filled with love. Today, being a nurse is a place of honor for me. It is a privilege. Being a nurse is a gift.

The Ruby Slippers

As did Dorothy in The Wizard of Oz, I too have discovered, there is no "over the rainbow" – there is only the reality of what is and who we are. There is no great and powerful wizard, no Emerald City, no magic bullet – all of this is an illusion. Modern medicine and science have their limitations – as much as we want there to be a great and powerful wizard, in fact, behind all of the science and technology of modern healthcare are imperfect, fallible human beings.

Take heart all of you seekers out there! We still have the ruby slippers – we all are wearing them, always have been, but most of us are not aware of this. The ruby slippers are the vehicle that will take us "home" – a place that we need to return to after all of our seeking "out there" is through. But nobody can tell us this, we all have to learn for ourselves what our ruby slippers might be. For me, the vehicle that has brought me "home" has been touch. Touching and being touched has brought me back in contact with myself and others – with my humanness and my limitations and with the limitlessness of love. Touching has demonstrated to me time and time again the resilience of the human spirit to heal itself.

Angry and disillusioned after my experiences with Christian Science, I put all of my faith into modern medicine. At first I thought, "This it it! It's great! I'm going to be a nurse so I can save people! Forget those religions, scientific knowledge is the answer!" then I saw the imperfection, the implied, unspoken demand for complete surrender to the system, for the giving up of personal power and choice. I then started going to twelve-step meetings and I thought, "This is it! Twelve-step groups are the answer!" But then I became aware of how I only wanted to be with people "like me" who were aware and living "consciously". A pattern was emerging – like quicksand, a black hole, that seemed to suck everyone in.

Then I learned the Rosen Method: "This is it! Touch is the answer, the ONLY answer! Everyone should learn to touch and everything will be great!" But how would this be any less elitist than my Mom's Christian Science practitioner telling her not to take pain medication? It is this mentality that separates us from one another – and from ourselves. How limiting!

Now I'm not saying that science, religion, twelve-step groups, alternative and complementary methods of healing don't have anything to offer us – on the contrary! What I am suggesting is that any one method, technique or expertise can and does tend to separate us from ourselves and each other. Not the technique, philosophy or method itself but the unintended consequences that too often befall the people who subscribe to a given approach. I'm talking about the exclusivity, the judgement, the arrogance, the "we have the answer and you don't" mentality that too often goes along with a particular method or technique – the self-mistrust and giving up of personal power to "belong," the feeling of rejection as an "outsider."

How would I sum this up? What would my conclusion be? What I have written is my story. The experiences that have shaped who I am today: someone that I have gotten to know very intimately and have learned to love, thanks to all who I have met along the way. The most effective "teachers" I have had have been those who have been a "gentle presence" for me, to hear me, see me and touch me. What I have learned, the conclusions I have drawn are how I see myself, others and the world today. Tomorrow it will change, I have no doubt.

Perhaps there will be something that you have read in this book that will feel right for you, something you might like to try. Maybe you've connected with some of the stories or feelings. Touch, it seems to me now, is a starting point, a stepping stone. Following, in the appendix, are practical, step-by-step guides for empowering yourself and others. What I have offered are suggestions only – try them on for size, adjust them to fit, make them your own, then let them go, remaining open to the unknown. You can have happiness right here, right now, in your present circumstances, no matter how grim things may seem, if you choose it. Those so called "negative" parts of yourself, those scary feelings, those "demons" are waiting to be invited for tea – to begin a "conversation" that will lead to your empowerment, happiness and health.

Neither a lofty degree of intelligence
nor imagination nor both together go
to the making of genius. Love, love, love,
that is the soul of genius.
—Mozart

APPENDIX

learnings and teachings

Learning to be a "Difficult Patient"

Shortly after my father's death, my sister and I met with his lawyer to discuss the will and estate management. Sitting on the other side of the huge desk, I felt both overwhelmed with new grief and somewhat intimidated by the lawyer's professional distance. In spite of my feelings, I asked him what percentage of the estate he took for his services.

He seemed taken aback and said, " I prefer not to call it *taking*."

"Okay," I replied, "what is your fee?"

Again, his eyes opened wide, his discomfort was palpable,"You're supposed to be bereaved!" he exclaimed.

Now it was my turn to be astonished. "I *am* bereaved, but I *still* want to know your fee!"

I was appalled at the lawyer's inference that if I were truly bereaved, I would not have even thought about how much his services were going to cost.

This very same attitude has been part of healthcare for too long and it's just the tip of the iceberg. We are expected to be docile, obedient "good patients" however, I highly recommend that you become a "difficult patient" instead. Here are a few pointers to help you or your loved one hone your skills:

- ***Ask questions.*** Ask your doctor, nurse or healthcare professional any questions that you need to ask, even if you think that the question may sound stupid or unimportant. Be brave, ask anyway. Making a list of questions and concerns that you want to go over with your doctor will help you cover all that you need to know.

- *Trust yourself first.* While there is nothing more important than our health, many patients have blind faith in modern medicine. Having trust is wonderful, but trust has to be earned. As you know, some people are not trustworthy; since doctors and other healthcare professionals are people, too, you can assume that the healing profession will have its share of untrustworthy individuals. Higher education does not automatically give a person higher values and morals. As a patient, you need to trust in your own ability and judgment to make informed choices that are right for you.

- *Make informed choices.* Very few patients question their doctor's authority, yet to make informed choices about your care, you need to have much information. Ask for a list of the proposed procedures, diagnostic tests, operations, medications, medical equipment with descriptions, pros and cons, costs, what your other options might be, and what may result if you opt not to follow your doctor's course of treatment. Sometimes there is printed material available, if not, be sure to write down all of the above information so that you can refer to it as needed.

- *When it's time to change doctors.* If your doctor or other healthcare professional is not responsive and respectful to you and your questions, concerns or your need for a second opinion, be direct and honest with him/her about how you feel about this treatment. If his/her attitude continues and you still aren't being listened to or treated with care and respect, then it's time to find another doctor!

- *Wellness instead of illness.* Insist that your healthcare insurance company or HMO cover all, some or give credit or reduced rates for wellness oriented and preventative treatment, education or programs. Make sure that it is written on your policy in clear, direct language. As a consumer, shop around for a company that meets your needs and specifications.

- *Trust your intuition and listen to your body.* If a doctor or other healthcare professional or their suggested course of treatment doesn't "feel" right to you either before the treatment starts, or after it begins you have a right to stop or change the treatment plan and/or the doctor. You don't need an explanation or a justification – It's your life, it's your body. It's your choice.

- *Choosing a new doctor.* Ask friends or family for names of doctors that they like. You may also ask the local hospital, heart or lung associations or other medical organizations for names. Call the various doctors offices and tell the receptionist that you are looking for a new doctor and would like to interview the doctor. You may not be able to do this in person, though that would be ideal, but speaking with the doctor over the phone and asking a few key questions would give you a pretty good idea as to whether you would want this person as your doctor. Again, write down the questions you want to ask.

- *What a "difficult patient" is not.* There is a fine line between being assertive and self-respecting and being demanding, controlling and belligerent. If you want to be respected and understood, start by being respectful and understanding.Your doctor or other healthcare professional has knowledge and skills that can be beneficial to you if you can develop a mutual trust and respect for one another. Be honest with yourself and your doctor, take his/her suggestions seriously into consideration.

- *Who's in control here?* It's your choice. When you are ill, you experience many feelings, among them is one of loss of control. And though it's difficult, it's important to be clear on what can and can't be controlled. You may feel that your body is betraying you and that your doctor is letting you down and those are both legitimate feelings but your response to those feelings is your choice. You could choose to be angry at and blame your body and your doctor – and then you are stuck in a lose/lose situation because you are now rejecting any wisdom your doctor or your body may have to offer. Or you could choose to explore how it feels to experience "loss of control" – frightening, isn't it? Accept that you are scared – acknowledge this fear to yourself and your doctor and you are now in a win/win situation – you have let go of the struggle and are now open to wisdom from within yourself and from around you.

CHOOSING A HEALTHCARE PROFESSIONAL...

If you are told that the doctor or other healthcare professional that you want to interview does not have time to call you back for a phone interview, or does not "do" phone interviews, ask the receptionist the reason. Is this doctor the kind that spends lots of time with patients and so is rushed between them and falls behind with appointment times? Does this healthcare professional have too many patients to handle or does he just not believe in patients interviewing prospective doctors? Depending on the responses, your priorities and what you've heard about this doctor, you may or may not want to set up and pay for an interview appointment.

The following is a list of some questions you may want to ask when choosing a doctor or other healthcare professional. Or use these as starting places to give you ideas about what matters to you.Think about or write down what is important to you and form your own questions to fit your priorities. As suggested before, have your questions written out so you remember to cover all that you want to and jot down the responses you get so you can refer back to them.

1) I believe in taking responsibility for my health and making the choices regarding my health once I have all of the facts. How do you feel about that?

2) If I were your patient, would you be open to and supportive of me seeking complementary therapy such as bodywork, massage, nutritional counseling, acupuncture (add your own therapy here) in conjunction with your treatment? Would you be open to discussing these complementary therapies with me?

3) If I were your patient, how would you feel if I were to seek a second opinion?

4) Do you take time to answer questions and explain proposed procedures and courses of treatment to your patients?

5) What is your opinion on the mind-body connection and illness?

6) How important are diet, exercise and mental health?

7) Do you feel that happiness and self-esteem affect physical health?

8) What kind of experience have you had treating (put your condition or illness here) and what kind of results have you seen with your course of treatment?

9) What are your strengths? What are your weaknesses?

10) Do you think that faith in God or some other higher source effects healing?

Pick only four or five questions or create your own, depending on your particular needs — you will get a good sense of whether this person is someone you would like to consider to be your health advisor. The next step is to make an appointment. Remember, nothing is written in stone — you can always change your mind at any time if you find that this person is not for you.

Note: If you have questions about costs, chances are the office bookkeeper will be a better resource than the doctor or healthcare professional.

Ten Ways You Can Help A Sick Friend or Loved One

Going to visit a very sick or dying friend or loved one in the hospital or at home can be a very difficult experience. Many times, people avoid visiting because the "don't know what to say or do" and later are sorry that they didn't go to see that person. This doesn't have to happen to you.

1.) Call first and be sure that when you plan to visit is a good time.

2.) Remember, you can neither change nor "fix" that person. Just being a gentle, accepting and caring presence is all that is needed. You do not have to DO anything.

3.) Listen, if they want to talk. If they don't want to talk, silence is fine. Don't chatter or engage them in conversation – it is tiring for them. If they doze off while you're there, that's okay, too. Just sit quietly.

4.) If you're comfortable, try this: ask if it is alright to hold their hand. If it is, hold it quietly the entire visit, even if they are silent or dozing.

5.) Do not console them if they cry. Tears are cleansing for the body, mind and soul, release stress and promote relaxation. Offering tissues (without them asking), or words like, "There, there, don't cry," though well-intentioned, can really be saying, "Don't cry."

6.) Encourage them to express their feelings, for example, if your sick friend or loved one says that they are afraid of dying, don't ignore their comment, change the subject or tell them, "Oh no, you're not dying, don't talk like that." Rather say something like,"That must be a scary feeling." This allows them to talk about it if they choose to.

7.) If they express anger about their condition, their doctor, treatment, the hospital staff, etc., you might state something like, "It sounds like you're angry." If you can accept that they are angry, you can make it easier for them to express, accept and move through their feelings.

8.) Pain is subjective. Even though you, or someone else you know, may have had the same surgery or illness, everyone's experience is completely different. If they choose to talk about their pain, allow them to feel it and express it by accepting and believing that they do hurt. Do not minimize someone else's pain.

9.) Be honest. If they ask you for feedback, be as honest as you can be. Do not give advice, rather speak in the first person. If you are feeling sad or scared, express those feelings. If you feel that you should be DOING something for them, you might say, "I'm feeling helpless." If you don't know what to say, state that.

10.) Do this ONLY if you are comfortable, feel it's appropriate and you have asked and your friend or loved one agrees: Try gently laying your hand on an area that they say is painful or tense. Just make gentle contact, without expectations, by touching that person as you would a newborn baby. Do not massage, push, pull or manipulate. Gentle contact with one or both hands is all that is needed. If your friend or loved one does not want to be touched, or asks you to stop at any time, honor their wishes.

Note: If your friend or loved one is confused, verbally unresponsive or in a coma, holding a hand or gentle touch is appropriate. Talk quietly and honestly with that person. Even though they may not respond, there have been many instances of recovered patients who have reported hearing their loved ones' words and feeling their touch while in comas.

How to Touch

When we touch someone, a change occurs. It's as simple as that. There is no magic nor mystery. I have learned that technique, though helpful, is really not as important as how we, as the "giver," approach the other person who is the "receiver." Of course the question that I'm asked very often (and what I had to know when I first experienced touch) was HOW DO YOU DO IT?

There weren't books on "How To" do the Rosen Work nor many of the other modalities that I studied and, for me, learning was (and is) all about hands-on experience. From the experiences, I took in what was right for me and, combining that with who I was then and who I was becoming, made it my own. Though I teach Touch, my students all have their own unique approach to the work.

So, be gentle with yourself and those you touch. In essence Touch is about being a gentle presence, a witness to the unfolding of another human being.

A Quiet Place: Ideally, work in a quiet place where you won't be disturbed by other people, ringing phones and outside noises. (However, you can still Touch no matter where you may be.) Soft music is okay unless it is distracting for giver or receiver.

A Comfortable Position: Have the receiver lie on a massage table, bed, floor, or sit comfortably in a chair. Use a pillow under the knees when lying face up, under the ankles when lying face down, to take the stress off of the lower back. Make sure that you, as the giver, are working so that you are also comfortable.

Dressed or Draped: Receivers may be clothed (loosening restrictive clothing) or undressed and draped with a sheet or blanket, depending on their comfort level. Skin to skin contact is best for the giver to detect skin temperature and other subtle changes.

Where to Touch: Ask the person receiving where they need to be touched. Are there areas of pain or tension that she is aware of? If not, does he have any area that bothers him from time to time? If the receiver states that she has no areas that trouble her, ask what she is hoping to get out of being touched or just place your hand or hands on an area that you may be curious about. Perhaps you notice tension in their shoulders or jaw or they have an area disproportional to the rest of the body. Simply begin.

Constant, Gentle Contact: Gently place your hand or hands on one of the areas that need attention — no need to push, pull or manipulate, just let your hand remain quiet and in contact with the body and if that area softens follow it in as deeply as the body will let you. If the body tightens up it may push your hand back — that's fine, remain in gentle contact, giving the body the space that it needs.

The Breath: Watch the breath — try following the body as it breathes in and out — keeping in constant gentle contact. (Try letting your breath follow that of the person you are touching and become aware of the area in your own body that you are touching on the receiver's body.) Notice where the breath is in the body you are touching and where it isn't. Are the breaths deep and relaxed, held or rapid and shallow? What might this indicate? (Example: When are breaths rapid and shallow? When we're afraid, excited or angry.)

Gateway to the Unconscious: The diaphragm is the muscle that is just under the ribs, above the abdomen that works with the lungs — it is both a voluntary and involuntary muscle in the body so it is controlled both consciously and unconsciously — it's a good place to put your hands and/or to watch for changes as it has been called the "door to the unconscious".

Becoming Sherlock Holmes: Let your curiosity guide you: look for "clues" the body gives you. Notice how that person feels under your hands — is that area rigid like steel or like rubber? Does it tremble, pulsate or is it still? What is your impression of what you feel, see and hear? Let him know what you are sensing. Ask questions of the receiver, look, listen and feel for the responses from the body.

Body Awareness: Ask the receiver what he is aware of in his body —

address the body and its changes rather than the "story" . Example: You may notice that the receiver's body is very tight under your hands and that his breath is rapid and shallow — tell him that. Ask him if he notices that and then ask what that is like for him. Or you may see her chin trembling and her swallowing frequently and hard — tell her what you see and ask her what that is like for her. Basically, try to avoid questions that require a person to have to "think" about an answer but rather one that encourages them to use their senses on a physical, feeling or "gut" level.

Knowing That We Don't Know: As giver, "listen" with rapt attention to the receiver using all of your senses — and let the person under your hands know what you are sensing. Try to remain in the "not knowing", non-judgmental and in the present. If you find that you are uncomfortable, judgmental or your mind is wandering, just notice it and gently bring yourself back. It takes some practice.

"Look, Ma, No Hands!" If you find that you are trying to "fix" that person under your hands: pushing, manipulating with your hands, feeling frustrated like you "aren't doing it right" or "nothing is happening here" simply inform that person that you will be taking your hands off and you would like them to notice how that is for them – what changes they may notice in their body, etc. and the session can continue in this way as long as needed. Remember, even with your hands-on, you are a witness only.

Body Changes: When you notice a "change" of any kind under your hands, bring it to the receiver's attention – you may ask what they are noticing, where, in their body, they are feeling or sensing a change. When something is said or felt that has meaning for that person, there will be a change in the body. These changes are usually very subtle and it takes some practice to notice them.The person under your hands may not be aware of the changes and that's okay. Again, you don't "know" what the changes mean for that person, you only need to bring it to his attention. (Some examples: trembling, pulsing, hardening, softening, temperature and color changes, tears, breathing changes, pounding heart, twitching, clenching of hands or jaw, etc.)

The Pace: You may spend the entire time you have keeping your hands in one area or move them to another place or two. There is no need to "balance" the body or work symmetrically as you would in massage. Quiet, gentle contact with the body will help focus the receiver on her body, feelings and senses whereas moving hands quickly and from place to place is distracting. What's a better way to really experience a journey? A high speed ride on the freeway or a walk down a country road?

When Intense Feelings Come Up: When the person under your hands experiences intense feelings or memories that may be very powerful and/or frightening, remain in quiet, constant contact with their body. Remember, you are only a witness and did not cause their feelings. (Please refer to "Having Tea with your Demons: About Feelings.") You may need to remind yourself silently that the feelings the receiver is experiencing belong to him and notice what feelings may be triggered in you. I remind myself of the boundaries between myself and others very concretely, saying to myself, "Those feelings belong to her, those are not mine. I end where my hands touch her body, she begins where her skin is," and so on. I had a teacher who used to imagine she was wearing an "energy suit" that looked like a space suit and the only openings through it were to her heart, eyes and ears.

Ending a Session: When you are ready to end your session, let the receiver know that you will be stopping in a few minutes so that she has time to prepare. When you remove your hands, do so slowly and gently, and encourage the receiver to allow herself some time before she gets up and dressed. Leave her alone for as long as she needs and take care not to analyze the experience afterwards.

Doing Touch on Yourself: People often ask if they can do a Touch session on themselves. The answer is "yes," though I prefer to touch and be touched by another person and a "witness" may notice things we might miss. If an area of pain or stress is easily and comfortably reachable, simply place your own hands on that area. If not accessible, focus your attention and breath on the area that needs to be "touched." Notice what it feels like – what are you aware of about that feeling or feelings? Give yourself the quiet, non-judgmental focus and attention that may be lacking in your busy life. What might your body, that painful or stressed area, be trying to tell you? Listen to yourself with love and allow yourself to have and express those feelings you may be experiencing.

When Not to Touch: If someone is acutely ill or has just been seriously injured, be sure that they receive immediate medical attention. Touch may not be appropriate for someone who is mentally ill, so be sure that you know this information before beginning. Knowing that painful memories and feelings may arise during a Touch session, be sure that you, as giver and the person who is receiving, will be safe.

Finally, working on a family member or significant other is not as easy as working on someone with whom there is little emotional connection. This is not to say that you can't do Touch on them, just keep in mind that it is much more difficult to be objective when both of you have an emotional investment in the outcome. With family members, I just touch them without talking at all. If that person feels like talking, I simply listen.

Having Tea With Your Demons (About Feelings)

Vishnu and the other Hindu gods all lived in a big palace in the clouds. One day, Vishnu, who was the king of all of the gods, left the palace to go away on a business trip. That evening, a demon came knocking on the palace door. He was a hideous, frightening demon and so when the gods opened the door and saw his gleaming, yellow eyes and sharp teeth, they were terrified. Now this demon was the kind of demon that ate fear and so as he ate the fear of the gods, he got bigger and fatter. And the bigger he got, the more frightened the gods became. The demon continued feeding on the fear of the gods until finally, he was so huge that he filled the entire palace.

It was about that time that Vishnu returned and found the gods all huddled in one corner and the demon filling the rest of the palace. Now Vishnu was wise and he knew what to do. He offered the demon some tea, made himself a cup and sat down with him. Vishnu talked with the demon, listened to him and slowly the demon became smaller and smaller until finally, when Vishnu had gotten to know the demon, he had become very small indeed.

When Feelings Seem Huge: Sometimes clients tell me, "I'm afraid if I start crying I will never stop." I used to fear that if I really felt my rage, I would kill someone. Feelings of grief, rage and other so-called negative feelings that are "stored" in your unconscious for years and years, build up pressure, like the steam in a pressure cooker. They feel too big to handle and indeed, they may fill every corner of your being as did the demon who ate fear. Again, you are probably not even aware that you are storing these feelings in your body and unconscious until the physical, emotional and/or spiritual pain becomes intense enough for you to have to stop and take notice.

You Can't Selectively Feel: You can't choose to feel only the "good" stuff and not the "bad" stuff. You are either feeling and experiencing the joys and sorrows of life to the fullest or you are going through the motions. Unconscious denial of rage, grief and the other "negative" feelings also limits the joy, love and spontaneity. Perhaps somewhere along the way you learned that you did not have a right to feel certain emotions. I once heard "Depression" defined as "anger we don't feel we have a right to have."

You Are Not Your Feelings: Though your stored feelings may seem too huge to handle and appear to fill all of your being, they are not who you are. As with the demon who ate fear, your feelings seem so huge that all of your focus is on the fear, the demon and keeping him hidden from yourself and others. There is no room for you. At this point, you do not know who you are. You believe you are your feelings and that you are being helplessly tossed about by them.

"Sitting" With Your Feelings: Here's the part where you can put on the kettle for tea. Though scary, you can offer your bigger-than-life feelings a cup of tea and fix one for yourself. (You just have to remember to put your cup and saucer on the table so that your demons won't hear them rattle in your hands.) Feel the fear and do it anyway. Through Touch, traditional therapy or whatever you choose, you can have someone by your side. You can use the "H" word – help. You will still have to feel the fear and do the work, but it is wonderful to know that you are not alone.

There are no "Unacceptable" Feelings: There are no unacceptable feelings only unacceptable behavior. As a child, when my Dad was angry, it was dangerous. He would drink, wield a loaded pistol and become verbally and physically abusive. I learned, then, that anger and potentially deadly behavior were one and the same. On a "gut" level, unconsciously the feeling and the behavior were not separate and so if I or someone else was angry, it could be deadly. I had to learn that when I was angry, I could choose if, how and when I would express it.

The Feelings of Others: Besides separating the feeling and the behavior, define which feelings are clearly your own and which belong to others. As your family, friends, co-workers and others express their feelings, they may not always take ownership.They may blame you for causing their anger, pain, discomfort etc. and certainly, if you have said or done something to hurt them, you need to take responsibility for your part. Conversely, you would hope that others would do the same. This, however is not always the case. Again, you need to own what is yours (even if it's just to yourself) and step back, recognizing that you do not have to react to, or be "pulled in" to someone else's rage, blame, grief, etc. You can choose to remain a gentle presence for them (as long as you are not being abused by them in any way) acknowledging their feelings and your own. Here you can help another, if they allow it, by putting on the tea for that person and his demons, as a loving witness.

Overreacting: If you find that you respond to life's little irritations with irrational rage or to sad movies and events with inconsolable grief, you are probably holding on to old pain that needs to be invited to tea.

Sounds of Silence: Silence is interesting. Most of us have a tough time sitting quietly, even those of us who aren't constantly on the go physically, still have minds and mouths that are in perpetual motion. Just like a hyperactive child, you may be acting out by cluttering your mind and life with "busy-ness" You may use alcohol, food, work, sex, drugs or any number of distractions that keep the focus off of yourself and keep you from feeling the fear and the pain. Touching another gives both giver and receiver time to BE in the present, to BE WITH the feelings, to sit and listen with all of your senses. Acknowledging first, then owning your demons will move you towards acceptance and love of yourself and then others. True feelings are quiet and deep, and once known you will find them to be part of what makes you a truly lovable human being.

Ten Truths About Tears

I never cry. - If you find that you feel unmoved and distant from life, you don't feel particularly sad but you experience no joy, like you are wearing a mask and are only "going through the motions" of living, you may be out of touch with stored feelings of grief.

Everything makes me cry. - Do you cry at every sad movie and for seemingly no reason at all? You also may be storing grief that needs to be acknowledged and explored. Crying at the drop of a hat for others, for circumstances around you, or for the state of the world may be another way of distancing yourself from your own deep feelings of grief and loss. The focus is on the world around you and how everything makes you cry rather than recognizing and claiming the pain as your own.

1) *Sad tears, glad tears.* Tears are the expression of feelings of joy as well as sadness and need to flow. Crying and laughing cause the same positive physiological changes in the body.

2) *Holding back the tears.* If tears are held back, they do not dissipate but rather are stored up, much like river water behind a dam. As time goes by and the pressure builds, all of your energy and focus goes in to keeping the dam from breaking. No or low energy and accompanying depression is one of the most widespread complaints from patients.

3) *Where tears are stored.* Areas in the body where tears are often stored are the neck, throat and upper chest. Pay attention to those areas – are they tight or painful? Sinus problems or infections may also be connected to unshed tears.

4) *Behind the tears.* Do you use tears to get the attention of others?

Out of the frustration of feeling powerless and/or to control others? To get what you want? You need to own the true feelings behind the tears. What keeps you from asking for what you want? What keeps you from wanting?

5) *The grief-anger connection.* Want to know where the "hidden grief" may be? Look under the anger/rage. It's all connected: I once heard that whining is anger through a very small hole and that depression is anger we don't feel we have a right to have. What does a wounded animal do? Attack! And what's under it all of the anger/rage? The deep hurt of grief and loss.

6) *You can't hurry tears.* If you find that you have grieving to do, allow yourself to feel it in a safe place and if experiencing this with someone present, be sure it is with someone you trust. Sometimes grief that has been stored up for years and years, needs days, months or even years to acknowledge and express. Be patient and gentle with yourself.

7) *Why cry?* You don't need a reason to cry. Like any feeling, you don't need to explain your feelings – you don't need to create reasons or circumstances in your life to justify your tears.

8) *You don't have to cry.* True feelings are quiet and deep – a single tear is fine – so is a simple acknowledgement like "I am sad" or "I hurt" without any tears at all.

9) *Tears are neither right nor wrong.* Tears just are. You don't need to analyze – just be honest with yourself about what you are feeling and open to the possibilities. When you take responsibility for and own your feelings, you reclaim your personal power.

10) *Try this visualization:* After reading this, close your eyes and imagine a small child about four years old. This little child is all alone and is crying, not a tantrum or whining but deep and heartfelt. What do you do? Now just give yourself some time to visualize the crying child and your response.

So what did you do in your visualization? Pick the child up in your arms? Ask what is wrong? Really listen? Or did you ignore that child, wish he would stop crying, or walk away? Did you figure someone else (the parents) should take care of her? Whatever your answer, that, most likely, is how you treat that part of you that needs to cry.

About PAIN

Why do people come for a Touch session or for any treatment or therapy? To get rid of the pain, of course. I will use the term pain here to also refer to tension, depression, disease and other so-called "bad", "negative" or "undesirable" conditions of the body, mind and spirit. I'm referring to chronic pain, etc. not acute pain and/or illness from physical trauma, burns, infections, exposure to toxins, etc. How do we do this?

Pain is not the bad guy - Pain is a symptom of something else that is going on in the body, mind and/or spirit – pain is the messenger. So don't shoot the messenger! Instead, listen to what that pain may be telling you. I call pain the idiot light on the dashboard of life.

Embrace the pain - By fighting the pain, denying it and pushing it away, we are increasing tension and struggle and that increases the pain. Imagine that your pain is a little child all alone, frightened and crying – embrace that child, listen to him, accept that he hurts.

Feel the Pain - Focus on the pain: what does it feel like? Is it sharp, dull, aching? Is it constant or intermittent? When are you aware of the pain, what is happening around you, in your life, in your thoughts when the pain is present and when it is gone? You need not DO anything, just acknowledge it. "Yes, I hurt." Like "kissing the boo boo," acknowledging the pain lessens it.

Experience the Pain - What are you feeling when you experience the pain? Frightened? Angry? Helpless? Indignant? Blaming? Is this feeling familiar in your life? Have you experienced these feelings before? If so, when? What are your beliefs and attitudes about pain? What has been your past experience with pain?

Own the Pain - Has someone hurt you emotionally or physically in the past? Are you still being hurt in your life now? What beliefs, attitudes and feelings do you have about yourself and pain that may be keeping you from moving away from the pain? What keeps you a victim? Only children and those people mentally unable to make choices can be victims. Taking ownership of the choices you have made in your adult life is a big step towards letting go of pain. Recognizing and acknowledging the pain you experienced as a child, when most choices were made for you, is another.

Rewards of Pain - Many of us identify with pain – we may have grown up with pain, it may have been all around us with parents that were in pain physically, emotionally and /or spiritually. Pain may be what and who we think we are. We may have learned early on that pain is what life is all about. Perhaps we believe, somewhere in our child unconscious that if we take on the pain, we can help our parents, feel we belong to or identify with them. Perhaps there is some guilt when we feel happy – many children are berated for expressing joy and spontaneity. Generally speaking, exuberance is socialized out of us as we grow up. Do we get attention and sympathy if we are ill or in pain? Do we feel in control when we get the attention and sympathy of others? Do we feel nobody could have possibly suffered as much as we have? Is there some sort of goodness or holiness in being a martyr? Are the expectations that we have of ourselves and those others have of us more lenient if we are suffering?

Holding on to Pain - There are many reasons, mostly unconscious, that keep us holding on to pain. So often, we are in pain physically, emotionally and/or spiritually and don't recognize that we are. What happens when we are in enough pain to take notice? We immediately want to make it go away. It's a natural response because it hurts! It's then that we try to force a change and declare war on our pain. But like a child that is holding on to a toy, what happens when we abruptly take that toy away? The child screams and cries, throws a tantrum and holds on to that toy as if his life depended on it. What happens if we say, "Okay, you can have that toy." and leave the child to continue to have that toy? Soon he will loose interest and let it go. Trying to force a change only increases the ferocity with which we resist the change.

Life is Not Pain - Though we all have and will experience pain and suffering in our lives, the words life and pain are not synonymous. Some pain we have no control over - it's unavoidable. But ask yourself: can you think of a time when you made a choice and had a gut feeling that there would be painful consequences? Have you chosen a relationship, job, living situation that has been painful? Chances are, if you honestly examine your so-called choice, it was really not a conscious choice after all, but rather a conditioned response, a reaction, a going with the flow or done to please someone else.

The Cry Button

Areas of the Body and The Feelings They Store

Peter, the Vietnam Vet, called the spot that I touched in his upper chest his "cry button." It seemed that every time that area was touched during a session, he would experience sadness and even tears.

Over the years, I have noticed certain areas of the body that store specific feelings. Though nothing is without exception, these are good starting points. Here are some areas of the body, the feelings that they often store, and some old adages and expressions that must have sprung from the connections:

Tears/Sadness/Grief/Vulnerability - Sinuses, chin, mouth, front of the neck and throat and upper chest, just under the throat. (Keep a stiff upper lip, keep your chin up, exposing your throat)

Rage/Anger/Burdened with Responsibility - Back of neck, jaw, shoulders, redness in the face. (weight of the world on his shoulders, pain in the neck)

Betrayal/Issues around Freedom - Upper back between shoulder blades, including shoulder blades. (spreading her wings, being stabbed in the back)

Issues around Love/Vulnerability/Love Lost/Open or Closed to Love - Mid-chest, slightly left over heart. (broken heart, cold-hearted, heartache)

Issues around Helplessness/Isolation/Asking for or not Asking for Help/Helping others - Arms, hands. (reach out, open arms, offering a helping hand, holding the world in the palm of your hand)

Taking in and letting go of Life/Fear/Hiding - Mid-chest and ribs, diaphragm area just below breastbone, just above abdomen. (it was inspirational, the patient expired, I held my breath, she breathed a sigh of relief)

Fear/Assimilation/Intuition/Vulnerability - Abdomen. (I had a gut feeling, my stomach had butterflies, that idea is hard to digest, a sinking feeling in my stomach, exposing the soft underbelly)

Issues around Sexuality/Mobility/Freedom - Hips, pelvis, thighs. (Ladies keep their legs together, he was stepping out)

Issues around Support, financial & emotional/Self-Esteem - Low back, spine. (he was spineless)

Issues/Feelings from Infancy & Early Childhood - Head, scalp. (pre-verbal)

Pertaining to the Female Side/Mother/Abstract/Vulnerable/Receptive - Any area that is left of the vertical midline of the body.

Pertaining to the Male Side/Father/Logical/Strong/Aggressive - Any area that is to the right of the vertical midline of the body.

Children

One Saturday I set up my massage table in front of a health food store at the mall to offer free demonstrations of Touch. An overweight woman approached me. She was dressed in wrinkled, ill-fitting clothes and her bewildered eyes appeared more so magnified through thick glasses which were held together with soiled, white tape. Following her was a silent, boy-like woman with a dull expression. She held tightly to a leash with a small child harnessed to the other end, whose antics and movements reminded me of an agitated monkey. The little dark-eyed boy tumbled and jumped, twisted and rolled so that his captor had to turn frequently to keep the leash from tangling around her legs.

The heavy woman, Evelyn, was the little boy's mother. Having just moved to the area, she was looking for a job and had few friends. She told me that her neck and shoulders were constantly painful so I asked her to sit on my massage table and I kneeled behind her to gently place my hands on her shoulders which felt like steel. Evelyn closed her eyes, leaned back against me and, in a little while, I felt some softening under my hands. She told me about the abusive marriage she had just left, about shame and loneliness and a single tear rolled down her cheek. Just then, her hyperactive son let out a shrill, piercing wail. Evelyn's shoulders tensed again. I glanced over to the boy whose frenzied movements had increased.

"Sometimes," Evelyn said, " I feel like I want to scream like that."

"It sounds like you are in a lot of pain." I responded.

Evelyn nodded. It occurred to me that her son was acting out her pain and I wondered what would happen if I touched him, too. I asked Evelyn if I could and she agreed. Unhooking his leash, I lifted him up to sit next to his mother on the table. Then kneeling behind Evelyn and her son, I placed one hand on Evelyn's tight shoulder and the other on Robby's. Very quickly, Evelyn again leaned back against me and closed her eyes with a sigh. Her body silently softened. To my delight and amazement, in less than two minutes, Robby had leaned his little body back against me, too and there he stayed quietly for twenty minutes, until our time was up. I had to keep looking over his head to be sure that he hadn't fallen asleep – he was wide awake. Robby just sat there serenely watching the Saturday shoppers go by, following their movements with his big, brown eyes.

Parenting — the Toughest Job: Being a parent is one of the toughest jobs we will ever have. It's all on-the-job training and as soon as we think we have one age figured out, they're older and there's a whole new frame of reference. If, as an adult, we have been able to keep those old painful, unresolved feelings of ours buried deep inside, it's guaranteed that when we have a child, there is no way they can remain contained. (Though we may still deny that those feelings truly exist, let alone belong to us.)

Parents' Unresolved Feelings: If our children are acting out, parents need to take a good look at our own unresolved feelings and attitudes. If we can learn to recognize and accept our feelings of rage, fear, grief, inadequacy, etc. as our own feelings and ours alone, we can begin to take responsibility and stop blaming this "lousy world" and our kids. When that happens, chances are, our children will stop acting out.

Children are not Clones: They are born unique individuals, we, as parents do not need to create what has already been created. They have a right to feel their own feelings and to express them. As parents, we need to set boundaries and guide them on acceptable behavior. There are no unacceptable feelings, only unacceptable behavior. How do we guide them on appropriate expression of feelings? By being an example.

Setting an Example: Let's change the expression "Do as I say, not as I do" to "Do as I do." If we want our children to be happy, we have to choose happiness. If we want our children to be honest and compassionate, we need to choose to live those values. If we want our children to trust and respect themselves, us and others, we must trust and respect ourselves, them and others. We also need to seek help when we need it from trusted peers and/or professionals and not "keep it in the family."

Children are not our Confidants: When we are overwhelmed, stressed or going through a crisis it is not our children's job to care for us. Though our children need to know (age appropriately) that Mom or Dad is not feeling well, upset etc. and certainly may help with what needs to be done, again age appropriately, we need to seek the help of a friend or, when indicated, a professional. It is not a child's job, at any age, to be expected to attempt to meet the emotional, physical or spiritual needs of the parents.

How to Change the World

Life is the same for all of us, some rain, some sunshine, we're all born and we all will die, yet why is it that some people, no matter what their lot, seem to enjoy their lives while others are miserable? Living joyfully and completely is not about changing the world around you but rather about clarifying your view of yourself and your relationship to the world and then, lo and behold, your world will change!

You are not alone: You may feel that nobody could possibly know what it's like to be you. That your feelings of isolation and despair are uniquely yours. Well, it's not true. Though others may have had different experiences than you, the feelings are the same. Reach out, open up a little – say the "H" word: Help.

Self-Love: You're okay the way you are right here, right now. All parts of you are lovable. Your anger, grief, fear, all of your feelings and imperfections are acceptable.

Separation: Though you have feelings, you are <u>not</u> your feelings. All feelings are acceptable and lovable but the behavior you choose in response to those feelings may not always be something you are proud of. Step back, observe what you are feeling, recognize that feeling as belonging to you, then make a choice and take responsibility for the behavior.

Ask for what you want. It's okay to want. Be honest with yourself about what you want and then ask for it. People are not mind readers and it's not wise to test the "If you really loved me, you'd know what I want" theory. You may not always get what you want, but you will never know unless you ask.

Control. Your children, spouse, friends and others all have a right to their own feelings. You have no control over and you are not responsible for their feelings. How others feel is no reflection on you. However you do not need to accept abusive or disrespectful behavior and boundaries need to be set.

Rescue. Not only is it impossible, but it's not your job to save the world! If you are a Mr. or Ms. "Fix -It," you have just been fired!

Being Human. You're not perfect, though many people try to be. It's okay to be human and make mistakes. There are no mistakes, just experiences and lessons.

Choice. Happiness is a choice, did you know that? Where you live is a choice, where you work is a choice, who you are married to or live with is a choice. Having or not having children is a choice. How you respond to a feeling or circumstance is a choice. You are not a victim.

Self-Care. It is okay to take care of yourself. In fact it's essential for a healthy, happy life. Start small: take a hot bath, buy yourself some flowers, say "no" to overtime.

Play. Though you are precious, you are not that important. In this world, 1% of the people love you, 1% of the people hate you and 98% don't give a damn. Lighten up and be silly. Laugh at yourself. Take time to play.

Empowering Others. You can empower others by looking at them, listening to them and touching them with your hands (if appropriate), your eyes, your voice, your humor and your love. Being aware and accepting of the fact that others as well as yourself, struggle with all of the above listed traits and inclinations is another way to empower those around you. When you empower others, you also empower yourself.

Being Present: If you miss "those good old days" or "are waiting for your ship to come in," you've just missed the boat! Life is right here, right now, in this moment. Give each moment your undivided attention so you don't miss a thing! Enjoy the sunlight shimmering on the autumn foliage, the sound of the rain on the roof, the crackle of a cozy fire, the taste of fresh coffee, the laugh of a child, a hot bath, skiing down a mountainside, the touch of someone's hand. Life is what happens while we're waiting for life to begin. It's never too late! Life truly begins at 30, 38, 42, 50, 88 (put your age here!) – Life begins NOW!

About the Author

photo by Tim Bezler

Linda Napier is a registered nurse, writer, poet and photographer who maintains a private Touch practice in Connecticut. Through personal and professional experience, she became convinced that health and well-being depend on nurturing, human touch. She not only incorporates this into her practice as a nurse, but also volunteers as "Daisy", a hospital clown, so that her patients may also be touched by humor. Linda presents lectures and workshops nationally on the topic of Touch for health and well-being and offers classes so that those who participate may learn to connect more deeply to themselves and others. *Tender Medicine* is her first book.